STRANGER THAN FICTION

• AGATHA •
CHRISTIE'S

True Crime Inspirations

Agatha Christie.

STRANGER THAN FICTION

• AGATHA •
CHRISTIE'S

True Crime Inspirations

Mike Holgate

First published 2010

The History Press
The Mill, Brimscombe Port
Stroud, Gloucestershire, GL5 2QG
www.thehistorypress.co.uk

British Library Cataloguing in Publication Data.
A catalogue record for this book is available from the British Library.

ISBN 978 0 7524 5539 6

Typesetting and origination by The History Press
Printed in Great Britain
Manufacturing Managed by Jellyfish Print Solutions Ltd

CONTENTS

Acknowledgements 7

Introduction 8

1 Agatha Christie: 'The Queen of Crime' 9
2 Jack the Ripper: Cat Among the Pigeons 16
3 Lady Nancy Astor: Appointment with Death 20
4 Lizzie Borden: After the Funeral 24
5 Sir Arthur Conan Doyle: The Hound of Death 28
6 Oscar Wilde: A Woman of No Importance 31
7 Agatha Christie: The Mysterious Affair at Styles 35
8 Dame Gracie Fields: A Murder Is Announced 38
9 Lord Carnarvon: The Adventure of the Egyptian Tomb 42
10 Sir Humphrey Gilbert and Sir Walter Raleigh: 46
    Dead Man's Folly
11 Robert Graves: Towards Zero 50
12 Madge Watts: The Claimant 53
13 Rudyard Kipling: The House Surgeon 58
14 Dr Crippen: Three Act Tragedy 61
15 Ernest Shackleton and Robert Falcon Scott: 65
    The Adventure of the Christmas Pudding
16 Billie Carleton: The Affair at the Victory Ball 68
17 The Sinking of the Lusitania: The Secret Adversary 72

18	Lawrence of Arabia: They Came to Baghdad	75
19	Eden Phillpotts: Peril at End House	78
20	Charles Lindbergh: Murder on the Orient Express	82
21	Frank Vosper: Love from a Stranger	86
22	Sir Christopher Lee: Murder is Easy	89
23	Dennis O'Neill: The Mousetrap	93
24	Klaus Fuchs and Bruno Pontecorvo: Destination Unknown	96
25	Dame Margaret Rutherford: Murder Most Foul	100
26	Roy James: At Bertram's Hotel	103
27	Lord Mountbatten: The Murder of Roger Ackroyd	106
28	Sir Peter Ustinov: Evil Under the Sun	109
29	Vanessa Redgrave: Agatha	113
30	Agatha Christie: Ordeal by Innocence	116
	Bibliography and Sources	119

ACKNOWLEDGEMENTS

The author would like to express his appreciation for access to archive material, illustrations, books, newspapers and online resources available at the John Pike Local Studies Room, Torquay Library.

INTRODUCTION

In the year of the 120th anniversary of Agatha Christie's birth, the ninetieth anniversary of the introduction of Hercule Poirot and the eightieth anniversary of the creation of Jane Marple, this collection of real-life crimes, scandals, tragedies and murders which influenced the works of the world's most popular author or affected the lives of many famous personalities involved in her career, proves the old adage that fact is stranger than fiction.

'The Duchess of Death's' fertile imagination was fuelled by the exploits of Jack the Ripper, which became the inspiration for the serial killings in *The ABC Murders*, whilst the kidnapping of a child in *Murder on the Orient Express* was based on the family tragedy that befell aviator Charles Lindbergh. Agatha was deeply moved by a horrific case of two young boys maltreated by their foster parents, which in turn triggered the idea for the world's longest running play, *The Mousetrap*.

Amongst people in the film world who suffered personal tragedy was Miss Marple actress Margaret Rutherford, whose father was committed to an asylum for murder, while Hercule Poirot actor Peter Ustinov witnessed the assassination of Indian leader Indira Gandi. The controversial twist in the plot for *The Murder of Roger Ackroyd* was suggested by Lord Mountbatten, who also arranged for his son-in-law, Lord Brabourne, to produce a series of star-studded Christie film adaptations before the two men became victims of an IRA bomb attack.

'The Queen of Crime' often used locations in her hometown of Torquay as a backdrop to her novels and, coincidentally, many of the true-life crime stories herein have links to her hometown, including the Profumo Affair, the Great Train Robbery and the baffling case of John 'Babbacombe' Lee – the only real-life butler to have been sentenced to death for murder – who became infamous as 'The Man They Could Not Hang'.

Mike Holgate
Torquay, August 2010

1

AGATHA CHRISTIE

'The Queen of Crime'

Take away the wolf from Red Riding Hood and would any child enjoy it? However, like most things in life, you want to be frightened a little – but not too much.

Agatha Christie (*An Autobiography*, 1977)

'The Queen of Crime', Agatha Christie, was born in 1890 in Torquay, the Devon seaside resort renowned as the 'Queen of the English Riviera'. The youngest of Frederick and Clarissa Miller's three children, it was at the family mansion, Ashfield, where she developed a love of detective fiction by listening to Sherlock Holmes stories read to her by her older sister. These experiences, linked to the nursery rhymes recited by her nanny, would later inspire her to produce a stream of classic titles including *A Pocket Full of Rye*, *One, Two, Buckle My Shoe*, and *Hickory, Dickory, Dock*. Although the celebrated author always retained the fondest memories of her privileged upbringing, where she was cosseted by household servants and educated by private tutors, her early life was coloured by a series of terrifying incidents, tragedy and sorrow that perhaps stimulated a morbid interest in death. This might have been viewed as an unhealthy fixation in a well-bred young woman; instead, it cultivated a penchant for relating murder mysteries that brought her critical acclaim and everlasting fame.

A decade younger than her siblings Madge and Monty, Agatha had an isolated childhood and invented imaginary playmates. Her closest friends as an infant were the family's pet dogs, and while taking one for a walk she witnessed the horror of it being run down and killed by a horse-driven carriage.

Tor Church, where Agatha Miller was baptised and acted as bridesmaid at her sister's wedding.

All Saints Church. Agatha was made a founder member by her father.

When aged eleven, further tragedy struck when she suffered the loss of her father. A man of independent means, American-born Frederick Miller had embraced the life of an English gentleman, idly passing his days visiting the yacht club or watching cricket and taking a philanthropic interest in local affairs. He donated money to the building of All Saints Church in his daughter's name so that she became a founder member. The fictional sleuth Miss Jane Marple, who made her debut in *Murder at the Vicarage* (1930), would have been proud of the parishioners of All Saints when they solved the mystery of lead gradually disappearing from the vestry roof in 2008. Volunteers sat up all night in the church and their prayers were answered and vigilance repaid when they summoned the police at dawn to apprehend the thief who was caught in the act.

In her autobiography, Agatha recalled that she enjoyed being frightened as a child and experienced feelings of 'indescribable terror' when playing a game with her sister Madge. They invented 'the Elder Sister', whom the girls pretended was mad and lived in a cave in the cliff face of the beach at Corbyn Head. Agatha enjoyed swimming but during her teens once got into difficulties and almost drowned at the Ladies' Bathing Cove. Far from experiencing sounds of music and seeing her life flash by, she began to black out as she sank beneath the waves, fully expecting to die, before she was plucked to safety by a local boatman who hauled her roughly aboard his craft and applied a crude form of artificial respiration – flushing the water from her lungs with a 'bit of punching'.

The fledgling writer's imagination was running riot from the age of four, when she experienced terrifying nightmares of a military figure she described as a French soldier in a grey-blue uniform, wearing a three-cornered hat over powdered hair and bearing a musket. His appearance would cause her to awaken the household by screaming 'The gunman, the gunman!' However, Agatha revealed that it was just before the age of five when she really 'first met fear'. This occurred when she went primrose picking near her home accompanied by her nanny. After walking up Shiphay Lane and passing the infamous White House of convicted baby-farmer Charlotte Winsor, who was sentenced to life-imprisonment for killing an infant in 1864, they entered a field and were warned off for trespassing by an angry man who threatened to 'boil them alive'. The panic-stricken child felt sick as she visualised herself being placed in a steaming cauldron – a memory that lingered well into old age: 'From that day to this I have never known so real a terror'.

Death became a commonplace event during the First World War when the newly married Agatha Christie qualified as a dispensary nurse at the Torquay War Hospital. Her knowledge of poisons and the presence of wounded Belgian soldiers inspired her to create retired policeman Hercule Poirot for

Corbyn Head Beach where the Miller sisters played a terrifying game, and the Grand Hotel where Agatha and Archie Christie spent their honeymoon.

Ladies' Bathing Cove where Agatha almost drowned.

her first novel, *The Mysterious Affair at Styles*, completed in 1916. Agatha had accepted a proposal of marriage from airman Archie Christie after attending a Wagner concert performed by the Torquay Municipal Orchestra at the Pavilion in 1913. The couple were wed on Christmas Eve 1914 and spent their honeymoon in Torquay at the Grand Hotel which, many years later, threw up an unsolved mystery that may have nonplussed the 'little grey cells' of her famous fictional detective. In September 1997, a guest was found dead in his hotel room. Having eaten a meal of roast lamb washed down with a bottle of wine and a cyanide-laced bottle of coke, he left an apologetic note in which he thanked the chef for a 'magnificent' last supper. Known as 'Mr Patel', the man had distinctive scars on his shoulders that led investigators to believe he had links with the Tamil Tigers, a well-known terrorist group. However, despite exhaustive enquiries neither his true identity nor the reason for taking his own life was ever established.

A milestone was reached in 1926 with the publication of a groundbreaking novel that many critics judge to be the crime writer's greatest work, *The Murder of Roger Ackroyd*. However, the year was marred by two catastrophic events. Clarissa Miller passed away and while Agatha wound up her mother's affairs at Ashfield, her husband remained at the marital home in Berkshire and began a love affair with his golf partner, Nancy Neele. In December Archie asked his wife for a divorce and, with her mind in turmoil, she drove off the road with the intention of ending it all but emerged suffering from concussion. She then abandoned her car and disappeared without trace. Before the amnesiac was located eleven days later at a hotel in Yorkshire, the derelict Ashfield was searched by the police in the forlorn hope that the missing author had returned to the sanctuary of her former home.

In an incident that would be replicated in a Christie play, *The Unexpected Guest* (1958), where the wife of a murdered man recalls her husband's irrational habit of shooting at people from a window of their home, the local constabulary had been summoned to Ashfield a few years earlier to caution Agatha's brother, Monty, who had ceased his illegal activities in the ivory trade and returned from Africa, having fallen seriously ill with a recurring infected wound received in war service. Considered to be the black sheep of the family, Monty cheerfully confessed to Agatha that he had led a 'wicked life' and fallen foul of the law all over the world, 'But my word, kid, ... I've had a thundering good time'. Although expected to live only six months, Monty's health gradually improved and he eased the boredom of his recuperation by firing his revolver at terrified visitors. Tradesmen and neighbours complained to the police but the gunman was unrepentant: 'Some silly old spinster going down the drive with her behind wobbling. Couldn't resist it – I sent a shot or two right and left of her. My how she ran!' Eventually Agatha and Madge

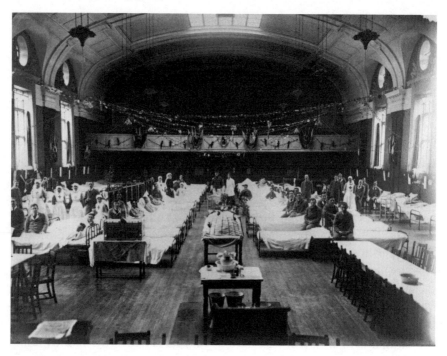

Torquay War Hospital, Christmas 1915.

Torquay Municipal Orchestra, Wagner Festival 1913.

provided their brother with a Dartmoor cottage where he was cared for by an elderly widow and mother of thirteen children, Mrs Taylor, whose own deteriorating health with bronchitis later necessitated further funding so that housekeeper and patient could make an ill-fated move to the warmer climes of the south of France.

Monty failed to reach his fiftieth birthday, succumbing to a cerebral haemorrhage while imbibing at a Marseilles café in 1929. The unfortunate Mrs Taylor died in hospital only a few days after accompanying him to France, having been taken ill with pneumonia during a railway journey on the Calais-Paris-Nice train which featured in the novel *The Mystery of the Blue Train* (1928). Agatha considered it her worst book, for she had written it in the depths of depression immediately following the collapse of her marriage.

When celebrating her eightieth birthday with the publication of her eightieth book in 1970, Agatha Christie revealed how her characters were often derived from real people and real places, while her rich imagination was stimulated from studying newspaper reports of true life crimes. Almost daily, distressing incidents of killing, vandalism, robbery and assault provided inspiration for plots. 'Could this be England?' she asked, 'And yet one knows how much goodness there is in this world of ours?'

2

JACK THE RIPPER

Cat Among the Pigeons

Confronted with the ABC murders, Poirot and his colleagues find it natural on several occasions to compare them with the Ripper's exploits.

(The Agatha Christie Collection No. 5, *The ABC Murders*)

In *The ABC Murders* (1936), Agatha Christie concocted a perplexing and apparently motiveless series of murders carried out in various parts of the country by an alphabetically-obsessed killer travelling by train and taunting Hercule Poirot with letters informing him where is he going to strike next – Andover, Bexhill-on-Sea and the railway station at Churston in Torbay. Alongside each corpse is placed a copy of the ABC Railway Guide opened at the page of the town or village where the killing has taken place. A strange, dishevelled character whose name is suspiciously formed from the first three letters of the alphabet, Alexander Bonaparte Cust, staggers into a police station believing he is guilty of the murders, but Poirot is not convinced. Before solving the mystery, the Belgian detective draws a parallel with the world's most infamous serial murderer in a conversation with his old friend and trusted aide Captain Arthur Hastings: 'Remember the long continued successes of Jack the Ripper'.

For *The ABC Murders*, Agatha Christie certainly drew inspiration from the celebrated true-life 'Whitechapel Murders'. They took place in the heart of London's East End, where homicide was commonplace, yet the sheer ferocity and savagery inflicted on the victims immediately attracted lurid headlines in the press as five prostitutes were killed and mutilated over a three-month period in the autumn of 1888. The first of these so-called 'canonical' victims

Churston Station featured in *The ABC Murders*.

was struck down on 31 August, when the body of Mary 'Polly' Nichols was found. Unable to afford a bed in a lodging house, she had been wandering the streets trying to raise money by prostitution when her throat was viciously cut right through to the spinal column, before her skirts were raised and her abdomen ripped open, exposing her intestines. A week later, Annie Chapman met a similar fate when her intestines were removed and laid neatly on the ground, while her womb was removed and taken away by her killer. On the last day of September, an infamous 'double event' occurred when two women were slain in a single night. Elizabeth Stride was last seen talking to a man 'respectable' in appearance less than thirty minutes before her body was discovered. This time there was no mutilation and blood was still seeping from the dead woman's throat, indicating that the Ripper had narrowly escaped detection. Forty minutes later, the psychopath struck again and killed Katherine Eddowes. With maniacal zeal, her throat, face and abdomen were slashed and a kidney and womb removed. The worst atrocity was saved for the final victim, Mary Jane Kelly, who was attacked in her lodging house on 9 November 1888. When a rent collector called on the streetwalker, he peeped through the window and spotted her naked, bloodied corpse lying on the bed. Her face had been brutalised almost beyond recognition, flesh removed from her abdomen and thighs was found on a bedside table, while the breasts had been sliced off and her heart extracted and removed from the scene of the crime. The shocked gentleman who made the terrible discovery remarked, 'It looked more like the work of a devil than a man'.

Jack the Ripper.

The discovery of one of the victims.

Letters sent to a news agency were signed by the self-proclaimed 'Jack the Ripper', and a prominent London citizen received a piece of kidney which the writer claimed he had taken from one of the dead women, while in correspondence purportedly received 'From Hell', he boasted 'tother piece I fried and ate'. Such psychopaths are usually compelled to continue their killing spree until they are apprehended, but following the death of the fifth victim, the murderer's reign of terror mysteriously ceased and the villain was never brought to justice. Since the time of the atrocities numerous suspects, accomplices and conspirators have continually been named in connection with the crime. These include: members of the royal family, Queen Victoria, Edward Prince of Wales, and Prince Albert Victor; prominent politicians Lord Salisbury, William Gladstone and Randolph Churchill; eminent artists and writers Frank Miles, Oscar Wilde and Lewis Carroll; and physicians Sir William Gull, Sir Arthur Conan Doyle and Dr Neill Cream. The latter was a Glasgow-born physician mentioned by Agatha Christie in *Cat Among the Pigeons* (1959), a tale of international intrigue involving an exclusive school for girls, where a character opines that the villain may be a serial killer like Jack the Ripper or Dr Neill Cream who 'went about killing an unfortunate type of woman'.

After graduating from Canada's McGill University, the notorious Dr Cream embarked upon a life of crime involving arson, blackmail, abortion and murder. While practicing as a physician in Chicago he was sentenced to life imprisonment for taking the life of the husband of his current mistress. Released on parole after ten years, he moved to London where he poisoned six prostitutes with strychnine-laced medication ostensibly administered to treat various ailments. Another would-be victim became suspicious and only pretended to swallow some poisoned pills given to her by Cream. She survived to tell the tale and gave vital evidence for the prosecution in the subsequent trial held in 1892.

Like the killer in *The ABC Murders* and the Whitechapel Murders, Cream was an indulgent self-publicist who enjoyed drawing attention to his crimes. In fact, he was the architect of his own downfall in Chicago where his victim was buried, arousing no suspicion that he had died from poisoning until Cream wrote to the district attorney suggesting that the body should be exhumed. Likewise, in London, Cream made an offer to name the 'Lambeth Murderer' if Scotland Yard paid him a substantial reward. Sentenced to death, without admitting his guilt, he seemingly confessed to a string of earlier crimes on the scaffold. As the hangman drew the bolt, the condemned man declared with his last breath, 'I am Jack the …'

3

LADY NANCY ASTOR

Appointment with Death

It was not often that Agatha Christie modelled a character on a recognisable person in real-life. However, you are tempted to identify Lady Westholme, the overbearing Member of Parliament in *Appointment with Death* who is 'much respected and almost universally disliked' with Lady Astor.

Christie biographer Charles Osborne

In the mystery novel *Appointment With Death* (1938), American Lady Mary Westholme is a domineering Member of Parliament married to a country squire. Although Agatha Christie claimed to have based the character on two women she had met in the Far East, readers could barely fail to notice the striking similarity with an American-born lady representing a Devon constituency, Lady Nancy Astor (1879-1964).

The beautiful, vivacious southern belle was twenty-seven years old with one disastrous marriage behind her when she met wealthy socialite Waldorf Astor onboard a liner travelling to England. After a whirlwind courtship, the couple were wed in 1906. Her friend, American cowboy comic Will Rogers, later quipped: 'Nancy, you sure out-married yourself'. She had a firm belief in the superiority of the female species and countered: 'I married beneath me – all women do'.

Waldorf had been born in New York on the same day as Nancy. His father, Viscount William Astor, had not endeared himself to his fellow countrymen when he moved his family to England in 1899, publicly stating: 'America is not a fit place for a gentleman to live'. Becoming a British subject ten years later, he took a shortcut to a peerage by becoming a newspaper tycoon.

The sinking of the *Titanic*.

In 1908, Waldorf entered politics. Refusing the offer of a safe seat, he became the Tory candidate for Plymouth Sutton, attracted by its historical association with the Pilgrim Fathers and America. Two years later, at the second attempt, he won the seat from the Liberals. During the First World War he served as Parliamentary Private Secretary to Prime Minister David Lloyd George before his career in the Commons came to end upon the death of his father in 1919. Waldorf inherited the peerage and was obliged to move to the House of Lords.

The part played by women in British society while men were at war had finally won them the vote and the right to stand for Parliament. Lady Astor became the first woman to take her seat when she fought a by-election in the constituency vacated by her husband, which she was to hold for twenty-five years. In her maiden speech she requested: 'I do not want you to look on your lady member as a fanatic or lunatic. I am simply trying to speak for the hundreds of women and children throughout the country who cannot speak for themselves'.

Her plea fell on deaf ears; the 'woman in the house' was mocked relentlessly, her presence bitterly resented in a hitherto exclusive gentleman's club with no facilities for women. Winston Churchill could not bring himself to speak to her in the Commons for years. When Nancy confronted him about his attitude, he replied, 'Well, when you entered the House of Commons I felt as though some woman had entered my bathroom and I had nothing to protect myself with except a sponge'. In *Appointment with Death*, Dr Gerard remarks, 'that woman should be poisoned… It is incredible to me that she has had a husband for many years and that he has not already done so', drawing on the famous exchange between Astor and Churchill: 'Winston, if you were my husband I should flavour your coffee with poison', to which he replied, 'Madam, if I were your husband, I should drink it'.

Nancy gradually overcame male bias. As a spirited opponent of socialism, a champion of women's rights and children's welfare, she won popularity as one of the most flamboyant personalities in British public life. When Nancy retired from politics at the end of the Second World War, the Astors had served the people of Plymouth for thirty-five years. Waldorf died in 1952, having supervised the reconstruction plans for the war-ravaged city. On her eightieth birthday in 1959, Nancy became the only woman to be honoured with the Freedom of Plymouth. She died on 2 May 1964 after a stroke. During Nancy's lifetime, the Astor family had been closely involved in two of the most sensational events of the twentieth century – the *Titanic* tragedy and the Profumo Affair. Coincidentally, both stories also had criminal links to Agatha Christie's hometown of Torquay.

In 1912 an inquiry into the maritime disaster which claimed the lives of 1,500 people was convened at a New York hotel owned by Waldorf, whose cousin John Jacob Astor was the 'unsinkable' luxury liner's wealthiest victim. The multi-millionaire's body was found floating in the water with $2,500 on his person. Giving crucial evidence to the inquiry was the helmsman at the moment of impact with the iceberg, Robert Hichens. Some twenty years later, he was the debt-ridden owner of a Torquay pleasure boat that was repossessed. After drinking heavily and brooding about his problems, he bought a revolver and shot the man who had sold him the vessel. Luckily, the bullet only grazed the skull of the blameless victim and Hichens was sentenced to five years imprisonment for attempted murder in November 1933.

Dr Stephen Ward, a central figure in the explosive 1963 political scandal, opened his first osteopathic practice in Torquay, where his father was the vicar of St Matthias Church from 1922-1940. After wartime service, Ward resided in London and treated the rich and famous, including Winston Churchill, Elizabeth Taylor and Frank Sinatra. He moved in high circles and, as a talented artist, was invited to sketch members of the royal family at Buckingham Palace. In 1956 he leased a cottage from Waldorf and Nancy's son, Lord William Astor, on the family estate at Cliveden. It was there at a party that Ward introduced married government minister John Profumo to showgirl Christine Keeler. She was also sleeping with a known Soviet spy, causing the society doctor

Robert Hichens giving
evidence at the Waldorf
Hotel, New York.

to observe there was the potential to start 'World War Three'. Profumo was forced to resign after lying about his fling with Keeler. Stephen Ward was then made the scapegoat for the sordid affair that had deeply embarrassed the government. Having supplied members of the social elite with a string of girls for sexual purposes, he was charged with living off immoral earnings. As the jury delivered a guilty verdict, the prisoner lay in a coma from which he never recovered, having taken a lethal dose of sleeping pills.

The most memorable moment of Stephen Ward's trial at the Old Bailey came when his former mistress, Mandy Rice-Davis, gave evidence. When told that Lord Astor had denied paying her for sex, she replied disarmingly, 'Well, he would, wouldn't he?'

4

LIZZIE BORDEN

After the Funeral

How sharper than a serpent's tooth it is
To have a thankless child.

Quote from *King Lear* used in *Ordeal by Innocence*

In Agatha Christie's novel *Ordeal by Innocence* (1958), there are two references to 'the Borden case'. For, like the crime in Christie's book, the real-life murders of Andrew and Abbey Borden appeared to have been committed by someone in the household. In August 1892, thirty-two-year-old Lizzie Borden raised the alarm after discovering the bodies of her father and stepmother at their home in Fall River, Massachusetts. The victims had been savagely attacked and killed with several blows from a freshly-cleaned axe that was found lying nearby. Police discovered that the day before the murders, two drugstores had refused to sell prussic acid to Lizzie, who claimed she required the preparation to mothball a fur cape. It also emerged that she had a clear motive for the crime, as she made no secret of the fact that she hated her stepmother whom she feared would inherit her father's considerable wealth. The only other person in the house at the time of the crime was a sleeping maidservant; therefore, Lizzie was the obvious suspect and was charged with murder after she was seen burning a dress, which she claimed, was 'stained'. A tidal wave of public opinion mounted against her, but by the time her trial was heard, sympathy had swung in her favour and there were joyous scenes in court when the jury announced 'not guilty'. The *Illustrated Police News* reported that 'the liberated prisoner fell into her seat as if shot when the verdict was announced'.

The verdict at
the trial of Lizzie
Borden.

However, people in her hometown were far from convinced by her plea
of innocence. Lizzie was ostracised by the community but continued to live
in Fall River until her death in 1927. Her body was then laid to rest alongside the graves of her murdered parents. One of the most famous unsolved
crimes in America, a theory has been advanced that Lizzie Borden could have
wielded the axe while having an epileptic fit from which she emerged with
no memory of the atrocity. Agatha Christie mentioned the crime on other
occasions: the Borden case is recalled by characters in *And Then There Were
None* (1939) and *Sleeping Murder* (1976), and a famous contemporary nursery
rhyme is quoted in *After the Funeral* (1953): 'Lizzie Borden with an axe gave
her mother forty whacks / When she saw what she had done she gave her
father forty-one'.

Another real-life case that developed 'after the funeral' was the case of
Sarah Anne Hearn, whose alleged method of poisoning was alluded to in
Sad Cypress (1940). The middle-aged widow lived at Lewannick, Cornwall,
where she cared for her invalid sister Lydia Everard until her death in 1930.
Sarah's immediate neighbours were a kindly farmer and his wife, William and

Annie Thomas, who showed concern for the bereaved woman living on her own and went out of their way to be helpful and friendly. In October 1930, the Thomas's offered to take Sarah on an afternoon drive to Bude and she made some salmon paste sandwiches that were consumed by all three people during the outing. On the way home Annie Thomas became ill and was later admitted to Plymouth Hospital, where she died two weeks later. When a post-mortem revealed arsenic in the dead woman's body, pointed remarks were made at the funeral by the victim's brother, who was convinced that there was poison in the sandwiches prepared by Sarah Hearn.

In response to these comments, the accused woman disappeared and there were concerns for her safety when items of her clothing were found on a cliff top at Looe. A letter posted to William Thomas suggested that she had committed suicide: 'Goodbye… I cannot forget that awful man and the things he said. I am innocent, innocent. But she is dead and it was my lunch she ate… When I am dead they will be sure I am guilty and you at least will be clear'. Far from being dead, however, Mrs Hearn had carefully planned her flight and journeyed from Looe to Torquay, where she obtained a job as a housekeeper using the assumed name of 'Annie Faithful'. Meanwhile, an inquest found that Annie Thomas had been poisoned by arsenic and an exhumation of Sarah Hearn's recently deceased sister also revealed levels of the poison in her body.

Alerted to her presence in Torquay by her suspicious employer, the police arrested Sarah Hearn, who stood trial for murder at Bodmin Assizes in June 1931. The prisoner impressed the jury by taking the witness stand and calmly denying that she had poisoned anyone. Furthermore, her defence counsel contended that arsenic found in Cornish soil had penetrated the coffins of the dead women and Sarah Hearn walked free, acquitted of double murder.

STRANGER THAN FICTION

Agatha Christie visited Iran many times when it was known as Persia and chose the location for a short story featuring Parker Pyne in 'The House of Shiraz' (1934). In May 2009, Iranian police arrested the country's first female serial killer and disclosed that the murderer's methods were inspired by the works of 'The Queen of Crime'.

The thirty-two-year-old suspect, named only as Mahin, was accused of killing six people in the city of Qazvin, about 100 miles north-west of Tehran. The prosecutor told Iranian journalists: 'Mahin in her confessions has said that she has been taking patterns from Agatha Christie books and has been trying not to leave any trace of herself'. Police said the accused confessed to killing four women in Qazvin, driven by a desperate need for money to pay her debts. Carefully choosing her victims, Mahin targeted elderly and middle-aged women by offering them lifts home from shrines in the city where they had been praying. After picking them up, the killer allegedly gave them fruit juice which she had spiked with an anaesthetic to knock them out. She would then suffocate her victims before stealing their jewellery and other possessions, then dump the bodies in secluded spots. One victim was beaten to death with an iron bar after regaining consciousness. Mahin also admitted committing the earlier murders of her former landlord and an aunt. Qazvin's police chief said that the accused was afflicted by a mental disorder. She would draw her chosen victims into conversation by telling them that they reminded her of her mother – who had deprived her daughter of love.

Mahin's killing spree was ended by a mundane traffic violation. A sixty-year-old woman reported that she had escaped from a light-coloured Renault car after becoming suspicious of the female driver. After checking vehicles matching that description, police attention was drawn to the possible identity of the suspect by records showing that she had been fined following a recent road accident.

5

SIR ARTHUR CONAN DOYLE

The Hound of Death

You know my methods in such cases, Watson: I put myself in the man's place, and having first gauged the man's intelligence, I try to imagine how I should proceed under the same circumstances.

Sherlock Holmes (*The Adventures of the Musgrave Ritual*, 1893)

Agatha Christie always felt a keen sense of rivalry with the creator of Sherlock Holmes, Sir Arthur Conan Doyle, the author she revered and succeeded as the world's most popular crime writer, for he had set a high standard by which all authors must be judged.

Arthur Conan Doyle (1859-1930) was born in Edinburgh, grew up in the city and studied medicine before moving to Plymouth for a short time in 1882. He briefly joined the practice of Dr George Budd, but resigned after observing the eccentric practices of his employer, who on one occasion insisted that he and Doyle throw plates of food at each other to cure a patient of lockjaw by making the sufferer laugh!

Setting up his own practice in Portsmouth, Doyle created Sherlock Holmes in 1887. The following year he applied a combination of his own medical knowledge and the cool logic of his fictional detective to a shocking real-life case in Whitechapel. In a letter published in *The Times*, Doyle suggested that Jack the Ripper might be a man disguised as a midwife who was able to commit the murders and walk through the district in a bloodstained apron without attracting undue suspicion. Doyle himself has been named as a possible suspect in the hunt for the perpetrator of the East End atrocities, possessing the necessary

Sir Arthur Conan Doyle.

medical and criminological skills to fit the profile of Jack the Ripper. The novelist has also been implicated in the alleged poisoning of two well-known personalities. The first case occurred shortly after Doyle returned from medical service in the Boer War, for which he was awarded a knighthood in 1902. Tired of the effect that crime fiction was having on his ambition to become an historical novelist, Doyle had killed off Sherlock Holmes in 1893 before bowing to public pressure to revive the detective hero in his best-known case, *The Hound of the Baskervilles*, written while he was staying on Dartmoor at the Duchy Hotel, Princetown, in 1901. In the book's dedication, the author faithfully acknowledged that, 'This story owes its inception to my friend, Mr Fletcher Robinson, who has helped me both in the general plot and in the local details'.

Journalist Bertram Fletcher Robinson, who later became editor of *Vanity Fair*, lived on the edge of the moor at Ipplepen and regaled Doyle with local legends of spectral demon hounds. The coachman who drove the pair around the district was the man whose name inspired the title, Harry Baskerville, who later claimed that Robinson had not received the credit he deserved for co-writing the story with Doyle. In 2003, author Rodger Garrick-Steele went further and presented a theory that Robinson was the sole author of the book and had been murdered at the insistence of Doyle, who was having an affair with his wife Gladys, whom he persuaded to administer lethal doses of laudanum to her husband. The symptoms of laudanum poisoning are similar to typhoid, which was the official cause of death when Robinson passed away aged thirty-six in 1907. Doyle, however, curiously contended that his friend, who had dabbled in Egyptology, was a victim of selective poisoning through the same so-called 'Mummy's Curse' that killed Tutankhamun-discoverer Lord Carnavon.

Doyle had a child-like belief in the occult, believed in the existence of fairies and was a champion of spiritualism – an issue he hotly debated in correspondence with Harry Houdini. The legendary escapologist fervently denounced false mediums until his death from peritonitis on Halloween 1926, although his great-nephew George Hardeen contended in *The Secret Life of Houdini* (2007) that no autopsy was carried out on the American showman to determine the cause of death. Furthermore, he contends that it was an act of deliberate poisoning by a group called the Spiritualists, led by Doyle, who wrote to a fellow devotee in 1924 that Houdini 'would get his just deserts very exactly meted out… I think there is a general payday coming soon'.

When Agatha Christie's car was found abandoned in mysterious circumstances following the shock of the breakdown of her first marriage in 1926, Doyle took an active part in the search to find out what had become of her. This was not by utilising the deductive powers of his fictional detective, but by obtaining the services of spiritualist Horace Leaf. After handing the medium a glove belonging to the missing writer, Sir Arthur later recalled:

> He never saw it until I laid it on the table at the moment of consultation, and there was nothing to connect either it or me with the Christie case… He at once got the name Agatha: 'There is trouble connected with this article. The person who owns it is half-dazed and half-purposeful. She is not dead as many think. She is alive. You will hear of her next Wednesday'.

Indeed, the world did learn of Agatha's whereabouts that day when newspapers broke the news that she had been found suffering from amnesia staying at a luxury hotel in Harrogate.

When Arthur Conan Doyle gave a lecture on 'Death and the Hereafter' at Toquay in September 1920, newly published author Agatha Christie was in the audience and rose at the end to propose a vote of thanks to the distinguished speaker. A year after Doyle's own death, she based the story of *The Sittaford Mystery* (1931) on Dartmoor where, in a twist reminiscent of the classic *The Hound of the Baskervilles*, a villainous convict makes his escape across the misty landscape in a supernatural mystery, where the plot concerns the murder of a man whose death was foretold to the hour by the spirits at a séance. Dartmoor was also the place where Agatha chose to complete her first success, *The Mysterious Affair at Styles* (1920), whilst staying at the Moorland Hotel, Haytor.

6

OSCAR WILDE

A Woman of No Importance

One could never pay too high a price for any sensation.

Oscar Wilde (*The Picture of Dorian Gray*, 1891)

Agatha Christie completed her first published novel, *The Mysterious Affair at Styles*, in 1916 but, astonishingly, the creation of Hercule Poirot, who used his 'little grey cells' to solve crimes, did not immediately find favour with publishers. Having been rejected by various publishing houses, the budding author had become a mother and virtually given up all hope of becoming a writer when, two years after submitting her manuscript, she was surprised to receive an offer from The Bodley Head. The managing director, John Lane, explained that he was taking a risk with an unknown writer but believed the work showed some promise and the relieved author naïvely signed a disadvantageous publishing contract which she would later regret.

During the 1920s the company relied heavily on sales from out-of-copyright works, and amusingly revealed that they had received enquiries from the Inland Revenue about the earnings of 'Mr W. Shakespeare' and 'Mr O. Kyam'. Before the signing of Agatha Christie, The Bodley Head's most famous discovery had been literary genius Oscar Wilde, whose spectacular fall from grace can be partially attributed to an incriminating letter he wrote in the birthplace of Christie, who was two years old when Wilde stayed in Torquay from November 1892 until March 1893. Wilde leased the villa Babbacombe Cliff from the owner, Lady Mount-Temple, a distant cousin and confidante of Oscar's wife Constance. Writing to Lady Mount-Temple whilst she was win-

Oscar Wilde.

tering abroad, Wilde commented, 'I find the peace and beauty here so good for troubled nerves, and so suggestive for new work'.

During his stay, Oscar completed the play *A Woman of No Importance* and supervised rehearsals of the first amateur production of *Lady Windermere's Fan*, directed by the Mayoress Mrs Splatt, which opened in January 1893 at Torquay's Theatre Royal. He also granted an interview to local history author and solicitor Percy Almy that appeared in the magazine *The Theatre*. Almy observed that Wilde had 'an engaging charm' which would win him many disciples and interestingly, in view of the scandal that was about to engulf him, recorded the great man's thoughts on criminals: 'Never attempt to reform a man, men never repent'.

Early in February, Constance left to join friends in Florence. Immediately, Oscar was joined by his close friend Lord Alfred 'Bosie' Douglas, accompanied by his tutor, who wrote of Wilde whilst staying in Babbacombe: 'I think him perfectly delightful with the firmest conviction that his morals are detestable'. Two years later, the relationship between Wilde and Bosie was to incite the boy's father, the Marquess of Queensbury, into denouncing Wilde as a 'sodomite'. Oscar responded by bringing an ill-advised libel case against Queensbury in April 1895. Produced in evidence was a damning letter written at Babbacombe Cliff, where Wilde had responded to a poem that Douglas had sent him:

My boy, Your sonnet is quite lovely, and it is a marvel that those red rose-leaf lips of yours should have been made no less for music of song than for madness of kisses. Your slim gilt soul walks between passion and poetry. I know Hyacinthus, whom Apollo loved so madly, was you in Greek days.

The plaintiff's case collapsed and he immediately found himself facing criminal charges on twenty-five acts of gross indecency, allegedly committed with a number of youths.

During the first of the two trials that were necessary to decide Oscar's fate as the jury failed to agree a verdict, Constance sought refuge from the press at

The trial of Oscar Wilde.

Babbacombe Cliff with Lady Mount-Temple. Whilst there, she wrote a letter seeking guidance from a fortune teller, Mrs Robinson: 'What is to become of my husband who has so betrayed me and deceived me and ruined the lives of my darling boys?' The lady had already given the answer two years earlier at a party after the London opening of *A Woman of No Importance*. Wilde was noticeably distressed when told that his right palm revealed that he would 'send himself into exile'. Indeed, after serving two years hard labour in Reading Gaol, Wilde fled to France, where in his own words he was soon 'dying beyond my means'. Loyal friends bore the cost of his funeral and one of then complained with unintended Wildean wit: 'Dying in Paris is really a very difficult and expensive luxury for a foreigner!'

The sordid revelations of the trials of Oscar Wilde resulted in The Bodley Head's most successful author becoming *persona non grata* and his works were withdrawn for many years after sales plummeted. The publishing company were to suffer another catastrophic loss when they allowed Agatha Christie to slip through their fingers by offering unfavourable terms. When *The Mysterious Affair at Styles* was published in 1920, the author received only £25 – a half share of serialisation rights that had been sold to a weekly magazine. No royalties were forthcoming until 2,000 copies of the book had been sold, a target not reached with the first edition. Furthermore, the publisher had a clause inserted in the contract giving them the option on the writer's next five novels at only fractionally better terms. Treating a new author like 'a woman of no importance' was to cost the publishing company dear as, unsurprisingly, Agatha quickly realised her worth and transferred her allegiance to William Collins & Sons. The first offering to her new publisher was *The Murder of Roger Ackroyd* (1926), an ingenious 'whodunnit' that was to become a sensation and substantially increase Agatha Christie's standing in the literary world.

7

AGATHA CHRISTIE

The Mysterious Affair at Styles

Loss of memory cases are… rare, but occasionally genuine.

Hercule Poirot (*The Disappearance of Mr Dagenham*, 1924)

In the year that she achieved her greatest literary success to date with the publication of *The Murder of Roger Ackroyd*, Agatha Christie found herself at the centre of a mystery as baffling as any of her complex works of fiction when she disappeared for eleven days in December 1926.

The case unfolded when Agatha drove off late at night, leaving her wedding ring behind at the marital home, Styles, in Sunningdale, Berkshire. The following morning her car was found abandoned with the headlights switched on near the edge of a quarry at Newlands Corner, a beauty spot on the Surrey Downs. Thousands of volunteers searched the area in vain for a corpse, before hopes for the author's safety were raised when her brother-in-law Campbell Christie received a postcard from Agatha, saying that she was travelling to an unspecified spa town in Yorkshire. It had been posted shortly after her car had been discovered. When enquiries in the White Rose County drew a blank, the police in Torquay became involved when they visited the author's birthplace, Ashfield. The house was found to be deserted following the recent death of Agatha's mother, a traumatic event that had left her bereaved daughter feeling depressed. However, the press began to suspect that the whole thing was a publicity stunt when Archie revealed that his wife had often said she could disappear at will and no one would be able to find her. He impeded the investigation further by failing to reveal that the couple had argued on

BERKSHIRE CONSTABULARY,
WOKINGHAM DIVISION.
9th. December 1926

MISSING

From her home "Styles" Sunningdale in this Division.
Mrs. Agatha Mary Clarissa CHRISTIE
(WIFE OF COLONEL A. CHRISTIE)

AGE 35 YEARS, HEIGHT 5 ft. 7 ins., HAIR RED (Shingled), NATURAL
TEETH. EYES GREY, COMPLEXION FAIR, WELL BUILT.
DRESSED—Grey Stockingette Skirt, Green Jumper,
Grey and dark Grey Cardigan, small Green Velour Hat,
may have hand bag containing £5 to £10. Left home in
4 seater Morris Cowley car at 9.45 p.m. on 3rd. December
leaving note saying she was going for a drive. The next
morning the car was found abandoned at Newlands
Corner, Albury, Surrey.

Should this lady be seen or any information regarding her
be obtained please communicate to any Police Station, or to
CHARLES GODDARD, Superintendent,
WOKINGHAM.
Telephone No. 11 Wokingham.
PRINTED AT THE "BERKSHIRE GAZETTE" OFFICES, PEACH STREET, WOKINGHAM.

A poster used in the
hunt for the missing
author.

the day of Agatha's departure after he told her that he loved someone else and
wanted a divorce. The police only learned of the couple's domestic problems
when they interviewed the household servants. The guilt-ridden husband
with something to hide instantly became a murder suspect and a week later
the pressure was clearly getting to him when he spoke to the *Daily News*:
'I cannot account for her disappearance save that her nerves have completely
gone, and that she went away for no real purpose whatever… I have been
badgered and pestered like a criminal, and all I want is to be left alone'.

Before Agatha was eventually tracked down to a luxury hotel in Harrogate
– apparently suffering from amnesia and using the name Mrs Neele – Archie
suggested three possible explanations for his wife's disappearance: voluntary,
loss of memory and suicide, informing the press:

I am inclined to believe the first, although, of course, it may be loss of memory as a result of her highly nervous state. I do not believe this is a case of suicide. She has never threatened suicide, but if she did contemplate that, I am sure her mind would turn to poison. I do not mean that she has ever discussed the question of taking poison, but that she used poison very largely in her stories.

However, in February 1928, Agatha gave an interview to the *Daily Mail* and admitted that dark thoughts of suicide had indeed played a part in her disappearance:

In my mind was the vague idea of ending everything... I went to Newlands Corner. I turned the car off the road down the hill... I left the [steering] wheel and let the car run. The car struck something with a jerk and pulled up suddenly. I was flung against the steering wheel, and my head hit something.

Up to this moment I was Mrs Christie... After the accident in the car, however, I lost my memory. I believe I wandered about London and I then remember arriving at the hotel in Harrogate. I was still muddy and showing signs of the accident... I had a bruise on my chest and my head was bruised... At Harrogate I read every day about Mrs Christie's disappearance, and came to the conclusion that she was dead. I regarded her as having acted stupidly. I was greatly struck by my resemblance to her and pointed it out to other people in the hotel. It never occurred to me that I might be her, as I was quite satisfied in my mind as to who I was. I thought I was a widow, and that I had had a son who had died, for I had in my bag a photograph of my little girl when very young with the name 'Teddy' upon it. I even tried to obtain a book by this Mrs Christie to read.

When I was brought back to my life as Mrs Christie again, many of my worries and anxieties returned, and although I am now quite well and cheerful and have lost my old morbid tendencies completely I have not quite the utter happiness of Mrs Neele.

Agatha's happiness was to be fully restored when she married archaeologist Max Mallowan in 1930, for there was to be no reconciliation when the Christies were reunited in Harrogate. The couple separated, then, when the divorced was finalised in 1928, Archie Christie immediately wed his mistress; none other than Nancy Neele, whose surname had been adopted by her troubled love rival during the author's desperate flight to escape from the reality of her marriage crisis.

8

DAME GRACIE FIELDS

A Murder is Announced

Miss Marple is a very popular with Agatha Christie's readers all over the Britain and America and it is a rather daunting task to try and play on television.

Gracie Fields (US TV guide, 1956)

Romance blossomed between Agatha Christie and Max Mallowan as they journeyed home from an archaeological dig at Ur, near Baghdad, travelling on the 'Orient Express' in 1930. When they arrived back in England, Max surprised Agatha by asking her to marry him. A whirlwind courtship resulted in the couple's betrothal occurring only six months after their first meeting – but only once the forty-year-old bride had come to terms with the age difference with her twenty-six-year-old suitor, a situation perhaps resolved by the old music hall joke, 'An archaeologist is the best husband a woman can have. The older she gets the more interested he is in her'.

The world's most famous train journey would later inspire the novel dedicated to Max Mallowan, *Murder on the Orient Express* (1934), and the same mode of travel was naturally chosen to transport Agatha and Max on the first stage of their honeymoon to Venice. Following a tour of Greece, the newlyweds parted in Athens; Max rejoined the dig at Ur, while Agatha returned to London suffering from a violent bout of stomach poisoning. Her journey home confined to her bed on the 'Orient Express' became a nightmare, but did not compare with a tragedy on the train that later brought an end to the second marriage of Gracie Fields, the first actress to portray Miss Marple on television.

In 1938, the Mallowans took the decision to sell Ashfield and move to the tranquillity of Greenway on the River Dart. Agatha was dismayed by the urbanisation of her hometown, which had experienced a population explosion as cheap travel made holidays available to the working classes. People fell in love with the resort and permanently left the industrial towns of the North to make their home in Torquay. One of the firms that pioneered coach travel from Lancashire to Devon was Yelloway, which grew from a Rochdale haulage firm launched by brothers Robert and Ernest Holt. At weekends in the early 1900s, the company would convert their lorries into charabancs and run trips to places of interest, including the ever-popular resort of Blackpool, before an unexpected opportunity arose to transport holidaymakers to Torbay. In 1911, a holiday was organised by a local printing firm for their annual staff holiday during regatta week in Torquay. Their journey was normally made by train, but a rail workers' strike necessitated the hire of a charabanc instead. Among the twenty-six people and one dog who made the inaugural 300-mile road journey from Rochdale to Torquay was singing sensation Gracie Fields (1898-1979), whose father Fred Stansfield maintained the vehicles for Holt Bros. The thirteen-year-old entertainer had already taken the first step on the ladder to fame by joining a girl's troupe until the vulnerable young girl was sexually assaulted and hospitalised for six weeks, suffering from a nervous breakdown that threatened her future in show business. Fortunately, the seaside holiday proved just the tonic and quickly restored her brash confidence as she kept up the passengers' spirits by leading the singing during the tortuous two-day journey. When the weary holidaymakers finally reached their destination, Gracie entered a talent competition on Paignton seafront and scooped the first prize of a purse, 10s and a pair of roller skates.

After continuing to tour with juvenile troupes, Gracie was made into a major national star by comedian Archie Pitts, who became her first husband. Her diverse repertoire included opera, ballads, hymns and comic songs. During the 1930s, she established herself as a leading film star in roles that recreated her own 'rags to riches' rise from mill girl to celebrity. Her screen debut in *Sally in our Alley* (1931) also provided her with the show-stopping song forever associated with her, 'Sally'. Her huge success led to offers from Hollywood and, following her divorce from Archie Pitt, she married her film director Monty Banks in 1940. During wartime, the couple came in for undeserved criticism for residing in America, a decision forced on them as Banks was born in Italy and faced detention as an 'enemy alien' in Britain. Gracie re-established herself in the nation's affections after the war and as one of England's best-known actresses across the Atlantic, she was chosen to introduce Miss Marple to the small screen. In a series of plays shown on *The Goodyear Television Playhouse*, the story chosen for adaptation was Agatha Christie's fiftieth novel, *A Murder is*

Gracie Fields.

Announced (1950), which was broadcast live from New York on 30 December 1956. Billed as: 'An edge-of-the-seat murder mystery featuring the Queen of Crime's famous lady sleuth', the production was not recorded for future showings and failed to impress the television critic of the *New York Times*: 'The mystery of the *Goodyear Playhouse* last night was not whodunnit – but rather why? Why, for example, did… Gracie Fields ever get involved in such an inferior melodrama? It was murder from beginning to end'.

Gracie Fields was fully aware of the historic significance of her one-off performance and in a television guide revealed her thoughts on the characterisation she had adopted to play the role of Miss Marple: 'I have always imagined her as a rather quiet lady with a quick turn of mind and a nose for murder'.

The music hall, stage, radio, television, film and recording star also made ten Royal Command performances and was made a Dame of the British Empire shortly before her death. Until the end of her life she remained a fervent fan of Agatha Christie and at her home in Capri, her library contained almost the whole the works of her favourite author. In 1950, a strange twist of fate tragically linked Gracie to a Christie story; while travelling to their island home, Monty Banks suffered a fatal heart attack and died in the arms of his wife travelling across Europe on board the… 'Orient Express'.

STRANGER THAN FICTION

In 1977, a severely ill nineteen-month-old child was flown on a mercy mission from Qatar to London for life-saving treatment. Her condition baffled doctors at Hammersmith Hospital when she was admitted semi-conscious and unresponsive to speech or commands. The next day at the routine ward rounds, Nurse Maitland, who had been monitoring the patient, put down the book that she was reading and surprised doctors with what proved to be an accurate diagnosis. She had been reading Agatha Christie's *The Pale Horse* (1961) in which thallium poisoning was described with symptoms that matched the child's. A laboratory test was arranged and ten times the typical amount of thallium was detected. The likely source was thought to be a domestic poison used to kill household pests which had been ingested by the child over a long period of time at the family home. Although the prognosis once neurological symptoms have set in is usually hopeless, the child responded well to treatment and made a good recovery.

9

LORD CARNARVON

The Adventure of the Egyptian Tomb

It is I who hinder the sand from choking the secret chamber. I am for the protection of the deceased.

Translation of the inscription on the tomb of Tutankhamun

Long before she met her second husband Max Mallowan, it is evident that Agatha Christie was conversant with the science of archaeology. Her many works on the subject first introduced an archaeologist into her collection of characters in *The Man in the Brown Suit* (1924). The novel featured Hempsley Cavern, which was based on the author's knowledge of one of her hometown's top attractions, Kents Cavern. Her father, Frederick Miller, had been a fellow of the Torquay Natural History Society which financed the excavation of the magnificent show-cave, uncovering outstanding examples of stalagmites, stalactites and evidence of prehistoric animals and human inhabitants. The author quickly followed up the archaeological theme in the collection of short stories *Poirot Investigates* (1924), drawing on a real-life mystery for 'The Adventure of the Egyptian Tomb', which concerns a strange series of deaths of the people who were involved in the discovery and opening of the tomb of King Men-her-Ra, an event we are told followed hard on the discovery of the tomb of Tutankhamun in the Valley of the Kings by Lord Carnarvon in 1922.

Agatha Christie had become fascinated by Egypt and its history during a three-month trip when she was accompanied by her mother for her 'coming out' season in Cairo. The experience inspired her to write her first novel, entitled *Snow upon the Desert*. The storyline featured characters based on

Kents Cavern featured as Hemsley Cavern in *The Man in the Brown Suit*.

people she had encountered in Cairo, with the exception of a deaf heroine. Although the work was submitted to several publishers under the pseudonym 'Monosyllaba', it was rejected and remained unpublished. When she finally established herself as a successful author, Agatha's interest in the Land of the Pharaohs was further stimulated by news coverage generated by sensational reports of the 'Curse of King Tut'.

During a landmark excavation, the tomb of the pharaoh Tutankhamun was opened by a team led by archaeologist Howard Carter and his patron, Lord Carnarvon. Among the treasures unearthed in the sarcophagus was the king's mummified body lying within a coffin of solid gold. The boy king was wearing a magnificent gold portrait mask, while fabulous jewels and amulets adorned the wrappings of the corpse. However, rumours spread that the tomb was cursed when Lord Carnarvon died a few months later from septicaemia, having nicked a mosquito bite whilst shaving. According to an oversimplified translation by the press, an inscription above the tomb pointedly warned of the fate awaiting the plunderers, 'Death shall come on swift wings to him that touches the tomb of Pharaoh'.

When the mummy was later unwrapped, a wound was found on the cheek of the pharaoh in the same position as Carnarvon's mosquito bite. It was also claimed that at the precise time of Lord Carnarvon's death, the lights in Cairo blacked out for twenty minutes, while back in England his lordship's dog, Susie, howled and dropped dead at Highclere Castle. Author of *The Hound of the Baskervilles* Sir Arthur Conan Doyle, a fervent believer of spiritualism,

Lord Carnavon and Howard
Carter at the tomb of King Tut.

believed that the tragic events revolved around 'elemental' beings created by
the priests of King Tut to guard the tomb. A more practical and scientific
solution to the 'curse' involved a theory that deadly fungus had either been
deliberately placed as a 'booby trap', or that spores of 'mummy- dust' had produced a harmful bacteria that was released on the unwary interlopers when
the tomb was opened some 3,000 years later.

In all, since the excavation, there have been claims that forty people have
been victims of the curse, notably Carnarvon's half-brother Aubrey Herbert.
He died in September 1923 from blood poisoning following a dental operation to remove all his teeth. In 1930, the 'curse' hit the headlines again when
Lord Westbury committed suicide following the sudden death of his son,
Richard, who had been Carter's assistant in Cairo. Furthermore, a young boy
was run over by Lord Westbury's hearse en route to the cemetery – a fatal
accident attributed to the evil power of King Tut. Although Howard Carter's
pet canary was an early casualty of the curse when it was swallowed by a

cobra on the day the tomb was opened – an event interpreted as retribution for violation of the tomb, particularly as a cobra was depicted on the brow of the pharaoh from where it would spit fire at the king's enemies – the archaeologist did not become a victim of the so-called curse and poured scorn on the intense media speculation, saying that 'all sane people should dismiss such inventions with contempt'. However, the resultant publicity raised the profile of Tutankhamun, who attracted far greater fame in a preserved state of death than he had achieved in his short life, having died of a sudden illness aged about eighteen.

In Agatha Christie's spin-off adventure, a similar series of supposedly supernatural deaths occur. Within a month of uncovering the tomb of King Men-her-Ra near Cairo, the head archaeologist and a wealthy supporter die of seemingly natural causes, a third member of the team shoots himself and a museum curator dies from tetanus poisoning. Hercule Poirot and Captain Hastings are called upon to investigate the strange affair and despite the clues pointing to the existence of an evil curse, the deaths turn out to be the work of a very real, modern-day murderer.

10

SIR HUMPHREY GILBERT
AND SIR WALTER RALEIGH

Dead Man's Folly

Greenway House, on the Dart, a house that my mother had always said, and I had thought also, was the most perfect of the various properties on the Dart.

Agatha Christie (*An Autobiography*, 1977)

In 1938, Agatha Christie parted with her beloved family home Ashfield and purchased what she had long viewed as her favourite property on the River Dart, Greenway House, a few miles from Torquay near the village of Galmpton. The historic thirty-five-acre estate had once been associated with two of the most famous seafarers of the Elizabethan age, whose lives ended in tragic circumstances: Sir Humphrey Gilbert and Sir Walter Raleigh.

Remembered as 'the Father of Colonisation', Elizabethan soldier and explorer Humphrey Gilbert (1539-1583) was born at Greenway Court. Educated at Eton and Oxford, Gilbert had a distinguished military career in the service of Queen Elizabeth before turning his ambitions to exploration. He advocated both the search for a trade route via a north-west passage over America to the Pacific Ocean, and also plans for the colonisation of the New World to alleviate the rising tide of vagrancy and poverty in the mother country. In 1578, Gilbert took part in a joint venture with his younger half-brother, Walter Raleigh (*c.* 1552-1618), plundering Spanish vessels for treasure. Having proved his worth at sea, he immediately received a royal patent to seek 'remote heathen and barbarous lands'. After various schemes foundered through lack of

Sir Humphrey Gilbert.

finance, he finally gained sufficient support to set sail on a doomed quest with a fleet of five ships: the *Delight*, the *Bark Raleigh*, the *Golden Hind*, the *Swallow* and the *Squirrel*.

Leaving from Plymouth early in June 1583, the expedition sighted Newfoundland by the end of July; it had, however, already suffered the loss of the *Bark Raleigh*, which had turned back through a lack of provisions. Entering the harbour of St John's, Gilbert claimed all land within a 200 league-radius in the name of the sovereign Queen Elizabeth. He also imposed his authority on the local fishermen by securing promises of fees payable to him in return for leases for the continued use of fishing grounds. In late August, the captain of the *Swallow* refused to follow Gilbert any further, preferring to return to England, while the three remaining ships set off on a reconnaissance journey southwards along the coast to Sable Island. Within days, the *Delight* ran aground and sank, taking with her a collection of mineral specimens and newly charted maps of the sea route. Panic swept through the superstitious crews of the two surviving ships, who now feared for their own lives. Their concerns were appeased when a decision was taken to abandon the mission and sail back to England. Gilbert was confident that his relevant success would attract royal patronage to mount larger expeditions to explore the Americas, little realising that this was to be his final voyage. Having encountered a fierce squall rounding the Azores, his ship the *Squirrel* was engulfed by the sea and sank beneath mountainous waves. The captain of the *Golden Hind* reported that Sir Humphrey was last seen on deck calmly reading a book and reassuring his crew as the terrible storm raged: 'We are as near to heaven by seas as by land'.

Sir Walter Raleigh.

Greenway (top right) overlooking the River Dart.

According to legend, when Sir Walter Raleigh first introduced tobacco in England and was demonstrating the art of pipe-smoking to his family at Greenway Court, the sight of burning alarmed a servant, who threw a jug of ale in the startled smoker's face in a misguided attempt to put out the fire.

Brilliant courtier, parliamentarian, businessman, soldier, seaman, coloniser, explorer, scientist, philosopher, historian and poet, Walter Raleigh was one of the most celebrated men of the Elizabethan age. Sharing Humphrey Gilbert's ambitions to set up English colonies in North America, Raleigh won favour with Queen Elizabeth by naming Virginia in honour of the monarch known as the 'Virgin Queen'. In return, 'Good Queen Bess' bestowed a knighthood on Raleigh and enabled him to become one of the richest men in England when she granted him lucrative monopolies in the wine and cloth trade. Administrative posts were obtained in Devon where he was appointed Vice-Admiral, Warden of the Stannaries and also represented the county in the House of Commons. The death of Queen Elizabeth in 1603 brought about a dramatic change in Raleigh's fortunes. His enemies at court spread rumours that he was opposed to the accession of King James. The new monarch immediately ordered his arrest and Raleigh was tried for treason, declared guilty and sentenced to death. On the eve of the execution he was granted a reprieve and committed to the Tower of London. Here, he was allowed special privileges and lived in relative comfort, accompanied by his wife, son and personal servants, but was held for thirteen years. During his captivity, he conducted scientific experiments and undertook a daunting literary work, *The History of the World*.

In 1616, he was released and given an opportunity to redeem himself by undertaking an expedition to the Orincho River in Venezuela to search for gold, promising to find evidence of the legendary El Dorado. He was now over sixty and fell ill in Trinidad, which he had claimed for the Crown twenty years earlier. The rest of the party carried on without him, but suffered many losses when they landed on Spanish territory and were apprehended by a patrol. The expedition returned to England in disgrace and on his return to London, the Spanish ambassador demanded that Raleigh should die and King James complied with the request. For the last time he was escorted to the Tower. Brushing aside thoughts of suicide he resolved 'to die in the light not in the darkness'. On the scaffold, Raleigh's final impassioned speech lasted for forty-five minutes. The executioner was totally unnerved by the victim's calm demeanour and required two swings of the axe to sever the head from the body after the prisoner declined the offer of a blindfold and declared, 'Think you I fear the shadow of the axe, when I fear not the axe itself?' he enquired. 'What dost thou fear?' urged the prisoner, 'Strike, man, strike!'

Greenway Court was eventually demolished and replaced by a Georgian mansion that became Agatha Christie's summer residence from 1938 until her death in 1976. The idyllic location overlooking the River Dart was featured in her books *Five Little Pigs* (1943), *Dead Man's Folly* (1956) and *Ordeal by Innocence* (1958).

11

ROBERT GRAVES

Towards Zero

Wars don't change except in name;
The next one must go just the same,
And new foul tricks unguessed before,
Will win and justify this War.

Robert Graves (extract from 'The Next War', 1918)

Eminent poet and novelist Robert Graves (1895-1985) was involved in some of the heaviest fighting of the First World War. While serving as a captain in the Welsh Fusiliers, he was twice mentioned in despatches and witnessed appalling atrocities which deeply affected his outlook; this led him to becoming an ardent critic of war, which was reflected in many of his poems. During the Battle of the Somme in 1916, the young officer was so badly wounded in the lung that he was left for dead and survived to read his own obituary in *The Times*. A year later he was hospitalised with shell shock and while recuperating prepared his collection of war poems, *Fusiliers and Fairies* (1918).

Throughout the Second World War, Graves resided with his muse and mistress, Beryl Hodge, in the South Devon village of Galmpton, at Vale House in Greenway Road, alongside the residence of Agatha Christie. These years were clouded by tragedy when Robert Graves suffered the loss of his eldest son, David, who was killed in action during the conflict in Burma. Significantly, at a crucial point of the war in 1944, the author's best known work, the historical novel *I, Claudius* for which he received the Hawthornden and James Tait Black Memorial literary prizes in 1934, was used as a plotter's codebook in an

Robert Graves.

abortive coup against Hitler led by a distant relative of Graves on his German mother's side, Count Claus Schenk Von Stauffenberg.

With the Nazis facing certain defeat following the successful D-Day landings in France by the Allies and a disastrous campaign repelled at Stalingrad by the Russians, several senior officers felt they had a moral duty to remove Adolf Hitler as head of the armed forces and install a government that would negotiate an honourable truce before their country was totally destroyed. As portrayed in the 2009 movie starring Tom Cruise, the plot was codenamed Operation Valkyrie. The plan was instigated by highly decorated war hero, Lieutenant Colonel von Stauffenberg, who had recently been appointed Chief of the General Staff of the Reserve Army after losing his left eye, his right hand and two fingers from his left hand whilst serving in North Africa. On 20 July 1944, the Fuhrer arranged a briefing at the Wolf's Lair headquarters in East Prussia, attended by von Stauffenberg, who before the meeting went to the bathroom and primed a bomb hidden inside a briefcase. Placing the device beneath the conference table, then leaving the room to take a pre-arranged telephone call moments before the explosion rocked the building; von Stauffenberg raced to a waiting plane and flew to Berlin believing that the assassination attempt had been successful. However, although four men lost their lives in the blast, Hitler survived simply because an officer had innocently moved the briefcase to the other end of the table. Although his trousers

Greenway, where Graves was a regular guest of the Mallowans.

were shredded, the Fuhrer suffered only minor injuries and later joked that his buttocks had been bruised 'as blue as a baboon's behind'. However, he was not amused in the immediate aftermath and ordered the arrest of those responsible. Retribution was swift and within hours von Stauffenberg and three co-conspirators were captured following a brief shootout and immediately executed by firing squad at the Berlin War Ministry. During the next few weeks, 5,000 suspects were rounded up and 200 put to death. The relatives of all the perpetrators were also arrested and von Stauffenberg's wife, Nina, was sent to a concentration camp. When still photographs of the executions of the conspirators were taken for the delectation of the Fuhrer, one witness recalled: 'Hitler put on his spectacles, eagerly grabbed up the macabre images and gazed at them for an eternity, with a look of ghoulish delight'.

When the Second World War broke out, Agatha volunteered for work in the dispensary at Torbay Hospital. Her husband Max Mallowan joined the Home Guard at Brixham before he was appointed to the Air Ministry in London, where the couple moved. They allowed Greenway to house evacuees until the property was requisitioned by the US Navy whose officers were preparing for the D-Day invasion of 1944. This was the year that Agatha's mystery novel *Towards Zero*, featuring Superintendent Battle, was published and dedicated to her 'friend' Robert Graves: 'Since you are kind enough to say you like my stories'. However, it later emerged that Graves's praise had been disingenuous – his true feelings about her work were revealed to be that 'her English was schoolgirlish, her situations for the most part artificial, and her detail faulty'.

12

MADGE WATTS

The Claimant

There is no doubt that Madge was the talented member of our family.

Agatha Christie (*An Autobiography*, 1977)

Agatha Christie's sister Madge, affectionately known as 'Punkie', was also a talented writer who had several stories published in magazines, including the prestigious *Vanity Fair*. Following her marriage to James Watts, Madge enjoyed what would be her sole success on the professional stage with a play that ran in the West End in 1924. *The Claimant* opened at the Queen's Theatre, produced by Basil Dean, who later founded the legendary film company Ealing Studios. Despite a cautionary note by the theatre critic of *The Times*, who commented that 'inexperienced dramatists are apt to be over-lavish with their plots', the play was well received and praised for its 'competent acting by an exceptionally choice cast', that included rising star Fay Compton. The 'hero' of Madge Watts's play is Roger Tunstall, a young man who returns from Africa claiming to be the rightful heir to a wealthy estate. It is based on the true story of an elaborate fraud which led to one of the most celebrated legal cases of the Victorian age – the Tichborne Claimant.

At the age of twenty-four, Roger Charles Doughty-Tichborne, heir to vast estates and a baronetcy, had a romance with his cousin, Katherine Doughty, until their proposed engagement was opposed by her family, who objected to his habitual drunkenness. Reeling from this rejection, the suitor resigned his commission in the Army and set sail for South America. He was last seen alive on the ship *Bella*, which was lost during a voyage from Rio de Janeiro,

The claimant.

Brazil, to Kingston, Jamaica, in April 1854. When Sir James Tichborne died in 1862, his second son Alfred succeeded to the title but his mother, Lady Henrietta Tichborne, believed that Roger was still alive and placed advertisements in the world's press seeking information about his whereabouts. In 1865 a reply was received from an Australian lawyer acting on behalf of a bankrupt butcher from Wagga Wagga known as Tomas Castro, who claimed to be the missing Sir Roger. According to the claimant's story, he had survived the shipwreck in a lifeboat before being rescued by a ship that landed at Melbourne, where he changed his name and started a new life. He later married an illiterate woman, Mary Bryant, with whom he had four children. When Sir Alfred died in 1866, his infant son Henry was the legal successor, but 'Roger' was summoned to England and accepted as the rightful heir by Lady Tichborne – despite the fact that his once slim figure had ballooned to twenty-seven stone. Furthermore, he had no recollection of where he had served with his regiment and had totally lost the ability to speak French, a language in which he had once been fluent. Following the death of Lady Henrietta in 1868, members of the Tichborne family denounced the 'claimant' as an impostor after making enquiries that revealed that Tomas Castro was in all probability Arthur Orton, the son of a London butcher who had emigrated to Australia and worked as a cattle rancher before becoming an outlaw suspected of involvement in murder. 'Roger' then launched a legal challenge to establish his right to the title.

The Tichborne trial.

The case was heard in 1871 and lasted 103 days, during which time the claimant had 100 witnesses to support him before the court, while his detractors produced 250 witnesses to testify against him. The trial came to a sensational end when the court accepted the testimony of Lord Bellow, who during his schooldays had been a friend of Sir Roger and tattooed his arm – marks that were not visible on the claimant.

The fraudster was immediately arrested and faced charges of perjury. Having no means to defend himself, he launched an appeal for funds and won popular support from mainly working-class people who embraced his cause, believing that he had been denied justice. The trial became one of the longest criminal cases in British legal history. Lasting 188 days, the defendant called 300 witnesses but it was to no avail; he was found guilty on all charges, declared to be Arthur Orton and sentenced to fourteen years imprisonment. Released on parole in 1884, the claimant's wife had deserted him for another man while he was in prison and he subsequently married Lily Enever, a singer he met whilst cashing in on his celebrity by appearing on the music hall circuit. A lecture tour of America followed but by 1895 he was reduced to poverty, forcing him to sell his story to the *People* newspaper in which he confessed to being Arthur Orton. He immediately retracted the statement after publication and used the money to set up as a tobacconist. Inevitably the business failed and Orton died in destitution in April 1898. Although buried in an unmarked grave at Paddington Cemetery, his coffin bore the name 'Sir Roger Tichborne'. This was done with the gracious consent of the Tichborne family, but did not appease a daughter from the claimant's first marriage. Using her 'stage name' Theresa Alexander, she continued her father's crusade and after pestering the Tichborne family with a series of begging letters, fell foul of the law in June 1913 by making a threat to murder Denise Grenville shortly before her wedding to Sir Joseph Tichborne, the latest holder of the contentious title since the death of his father Henry. The defendant was sentenced to six months imprisonment after writing, 'I am going to shoot that girl rather than Joseph marry her and they shall live on my money'.

STRANGER THAN FICTION

A short story collection featuring Miss Marple, *The Thirteen Problems* (1932), provided a useful 'recipe' for murder suspect Roland Roussell. A copy of the thriller, left open at the first mystery, 'The Tuesday Club Murder', with an underlined passage on poison was found at his flat in Créances, France. The fifty-eight year-old office worker poured an eye medicine into a bottle of red wine which killed his eighty-year-old uncle, Maxime Masseron, when he opened it on Christmas Day 1977. Roussel's aunt also consumed the potion and went into a coma. However, the arrested man told the police that the poisoning had all been a terrible accident as he had forgotten all about the bottle, which he admitted preparing the previous summer fully intending to murder a woman he believed had killed his mother.

Police were only called into investigate the incident when further casualties were admitted to hospital. The village carpenter and the victim's son-in-law went to the old couple's home to put the dead man in a coffin. The two men became violently ill when they helped themselves to the poisoned wine, which was still on the table. An hour later they were rendered unconscious and required emergency medical treatment before their lives were out of danger.

13

RUDYARD KIPLING

The House Surgeon

Torquay is such a place that I do desire acutely to upset by dancing through with nothing on but my spectacles.

Rudyard Kipling (1897)

The Miller family's status in Torquay resulted in them receiving many interesting visitors at Ashfield. Among them was Rudyard Kipling, the world-famous creator of the children's literary classics *The Jungle Book* and the *Just So* stories, and a future recipient of the Nobel Prize for Literature. However, young Agatha's only recollection of this momentous event were derogatory comments made by a friend of her mother's as to why the author had ever married his wife, Caroline Baleister, before reaching the conclusion that the couple were the 'perfect complement to each other'.

The Kiplings had also made themselves deeply unpopular in Caroline's hometown of Battleboro, Vermont, where the couple settled following their marriage in 1892. They left the country under a cloud after irrevocably falling out with the Baleister family. The quarrel resulted in Rudyard having his brother-in-law arrested for making violent threats, followed by a damaging court appearance and embarrassing publicity. In the autumn of 1896, the Kiplings left this bitter episode behind them and moved to England. They rented Rock House at Maidencombe, Torquay, built on a cliff overlooking a small cove. The author described the villa as 'almost too good to be true', and waxed lyrical about the location: 'I look straight from my work table on to the decks of the fishing craft who come in to look after their lobster pots'.

Rudyard Kipling.

With the publication of his latest work *The Seven Seas*, Kipling proudly accepted an invitation to spend several days with the naval cadets based on the training ship *Britannia* at Dartmouth.

Kipling's enthusiasm for his new home quickly declined as a sense of evil and brooding depression enveloped the household, which would later inspire a short ghost story entitled 'The House Surgeon'. He revealed a gathering blackness of mind and sorrow of the heart: 'It was the Feng-shui – the Spirit of the house itself – that darkened the sunshine and fell upon us every time we entered, checking the very words on our lips'. For a time, the writer took up the current craze for cycling. The gossip columnist of a local paper reported, 'I saw Mr Rudyard Kipling careering along the Tor Abbey sands on wheels one day last week'. The hobby ended when he and his wife shared pedalling duties on 'a tandem bicycle, whose double steering-bars made good dependence for continuous domestic quarrel'. The couple crashed off their 'devil's toast rack' and walked home pushing the bike they dubbed 'Hell Spider'.

Mrs Miller and her friend may have been unimpressed with the Kiplings, and likewise Rudyard could not bear mingling with the posturing, wealthy residents of the town, but before his unhappy sojourn on the English Riviera came to an abrupt end, Kipling fictionalised his Devon schooldays. Author Eden Phillpotts, famed for his novels set in the locality, sent a copy of his latest book to Kipling, which immediately triggered an idea. Early in 1897, he broached the subject with his editor: 'The notion of writing a Devonshire tale is new to me but, now I come to think of it, I was educated at Westward Ho! nigh Bideford and for six puppy years talked vernacular with the natives whose apples I stole. What will E.P. give to buy me off?'

The result was *Stalky & Co.*, based on the adventures of himself and his two closest friends at United Services College, an establishment fondly remembered by Kipling as 'the school before its time'. Founded to prepare boys for a military or naval career, this was never the intention for Kipling, as the college was chosen solely because his mother was a close friend of the headmaster, Cornwell Price. Despite a miserable initiation period at the school, which

Maidencombe.

he later recalled was 'primitive in its appointments, and our food would now raise a mutiny in Dartmoor [Prison]', the budding author flourished when the head realised, 'I was irretrievably committed to the ink-pot' and Rudyard was appointed editor of the school magazine. A collection of his poems written at the college was published by his parents living in India and he joyously returned to his family and embarked upon a journalistic career. He also drew inspiration from the land of his birth for his early literary successes. His output was stupendous and he became a marvellous storyteller, standing by the maxim that: 'A word – should fall in its place like a bell in a full chime'.

Kipling's revered former headmaster, Cormwell Price, accepted an invitation to spend some time at Rock House, where he heard passages from the new book read to him by the excited author. Kipling's happiness seemed complete when Caroline learned she was expecting their third child. However, by May 1897 the couple were unable to reconcile themselves with the gloomy atmosphere of Rock House and suddenly decided to execute 'our flight from Torquay' to seek refuge with relatives near Brighton. John Kipling, the son conceived in Torquay, was doomed to die in action during the First World War. His father had to live with the guilt of his son's fate after 'pulling strings' to arrange for his enlistment after John had been rejected on medical grounds with extremely poor eyesight. Little wonder that when Rudyard made a pilgrimage to his former Torquay home shortly before his own death, the writer detected 'the same brooding Spirit of deep, deep Despondency within the open lit rooms'.

14

DR CRIPPEN

Three Act Tragedy

I've always wondered if Ethel le Neve was in it with him [Dr Crippen] or not.

Quote from *The Labours of Hercules* (1947)

The plot of Agatha Christie's *Mrs McGinty's Dead* (1952), a murder mystery investigated by Hercule Poirot and Ariadne Oliver, is transparently based on the notorious crime committed by Dr Hawley Harvey Crippen, who was famously brought to justice when wireless was used for the first time in a murder hunt.

In 1900, the American-born dentist and his actress wife, Belle Elmore, had moved to England where Crippen's US qualifications did not allow him to practice medicine. Therefore, he took various jobs selling patent medicines. Ten years later he killed his domineering wife by administering a lethal dose of poison, then carved up her body and buried the remains in the cellar. The mild-mannered doctor explained Belle's disappearance by telling enquirers that she had returned to America because of a relative's illness. Meanwhile, he moved his secretary and mistress, Ethel le Neve, into his London home and when she began to openly wear Belle's furs and jewellery, suspicions were aroused and the police called in. A search of the house failed to throw any light on the matter, but the guilt-ridden couple fled to Antwerp and boarded the liner SS *Montrose* bound for Canada. Their hurried departure caused the police to make a more thorough search of the house and human remains were uncovered in the cellar. A torso was recovered but the head and limbs were never found and the body of Belle Crippen was identified by a piece of abdominal tissue.

DR. CRIPPEN, ENGLISH INSPECTOR WHO CAUGHT HIM, AND DIAGRAM OF CHASE

DR. HAWLEY H. CRIPPEN

INSPECTOR DEW

THE MONTROSE

The capture of Dr Crippen.

The execution of Dr Crippen.

With a warrant out for his arrest, Crippen tried to avoid detection by travelling under the name of 'Roberts'. He also shaved off his moustache and removed his glasses, while Ethel dressed as a boy during the transatlantic voyage. The ruse failed to fool the ship's captain who, observing the amorous behaviour of the couple, utilised the newly installed Marconi wireless system to radio an urgent message to London: 'Have strong suspicions that Crippen London cellar murderer and accomplice are among saloon passengers'. Alerted to the whereabouts of the runaways, Scotland Yard's Inspector Walter Dew boarded a faster White Star liner and boarded the *Montrose* from the St Lawrence River in the guise of a river pilot before arresting the fugitives in July 1910. Despite protesting his innocence, Crippen was tried at the Old Bailey and hanged for murder at Pentonville Prison in November 1910, while his mistress was tried separately and acquitted on charges of being an accessory after the fact.

Dr Crippen is also mentioned in *Three Act Tragedy* (1935), along with a reference to 'a man in the barrel'. This alluded to the real-life case of the defrocked rector of Stiffkey, the Revd Harold Davidson, who was prosecuted for trying to starve himself to death on Blackpool's 'Golden Mile' in 1935. Acquitted of intentionally attempting to commit suicide and awarded costs for false imprisonment, Davidson, a former professional entertainer, had been making a protest by exhibiting himself standing in a barrel and threatening to 'fast until death' unless the Church authorities reinstated him. He had been defrocked three years earlier when investigations discovered that he spent six days of the week in London and only visited his parish on Sundays. In the capital, the married vicar pursued girls with the religious fervour of an evangelist, although his motives were seemingly driven by sexual gratification. A Church Court heard evidence of how he had pestered teashop waitresses and lavished gifts on prostitutes. The defendant claimed that he was guilty of no more than indiscretion in his redemptive approaches to fallen women. Improbably, he explained that he tried to help the ladies he had befriended by paying for their lodgings and had taken one girl, described as 'feeble-minded', to Paris to give her an opportunity to 'get her a situation and pick up the language'. After a prolonged hearing lasting for several months, some charges were dropped, but Davidson was found guilty on five counts of immoral conduct and removed from the Church position he had held for twenty-six years.

Taking up the life of a showman to air his grievances about his treatment by the Church, his bizarre career came to a tragic end at the age of sixty-two while appearing at Skegness Amusement Park in July 1937. Taking his inspiration from the Bible story of Daniel, Davidson was engaged to address the public from a cage containing a 'docile' lion and a lioness, which were

The Revd Harold Davidson at the scene of his death.

normally fed and cared for by the amusement park owner's eight-year-old daughter. However at Davidson's first, and last, appearance, he was making a speech to an audience of 100 people when he stepped backwards and accidentally tripped over the lioness, causing Freddie the lion to protect his mate by springing up to maul the intruder. The victim was hospitalised and lapsed into a coma before passing away two days later. At the inquest, sixteen-year-old attendant Irene Summner was praised by the coroner for her bravery. Describing the accident she said:

> When Mr Davidson tried to get out of the way Freddie reared up on his haunches to get him with his front paws. I got into the cage and tried to beat the lion off, but it dragged Mr Davidson to a corner near the other locked gate and we could not move him until Freddie dropped him.

15

ERNEST SHACKLETON AND ROBERT FALCON SCOTT

The Adventure of the Christmas Pudding

Ordeal by Innocence… was inspired by a number of real-life heroes.

The Agatha Christie Collection No. 39, *Ordeal by Innocence*

In *Ordeal by Innocence* (1958), geophysicist Dr Arthur Calgary returns from an Antarctic expedition too late to prevent a miscarriage of justice. It transpires that he is the only man who could have verified an alibi and saved the life of a man who died from pneumonia in prison after being wrongfully jailed for the murder of his adoptive mother.

Agatha Christie's fictional polar explorer was inspired by two courageous men with Devon connections – Ernest Shackleton and Robert Falcon Scott. In August 1907, shortly before Agatha's seventeenth birthday, the supply ship *Terra Nova* steamed into Torquay on its last port of call before setting off on the first leg of an expedition to attempt to reach the South Pole. The leader, Lieutenant Ernest Shackleton RN (1874-1922), stayed behind in the resort for a further three months at his brother's home, The Knoll, before travelling on a liner to join his ship in New Zealand. The party returned to Torquay two years later having narrowly failed to reach their goal by less than 100 miles. The consolation was a knighthood, conferred by King George V on Ernest Shackleton. Bad weather and low rations had forced Shackleton to turn back within sight of his objective, but in view of the tragedy that was soon to befall a fellow polar explorer, he made a suitably 'chilling' remark: 'better a live donkey than a dead lion'.

Robert Falcon Scott.

Devonport-born naval captain Robert Falcon Scott (1868–1912) bettered Shackleton's achievement during an ill-fated journey to the South Pole completed in 1912. After successfully reaching his destination, he was disappointed to discover that Roald Amundsen and his party had become the first men to reach the pole only one month earlier. The Norwegian had switched his attention to the South Pole when American Robert Peary became the first man to reach the North Pole in 1909. Dejected and faced with severe storms and blizzards on the way back, Scott and his four companions perished from hunger and exposure only eleven miles from the safety of a food and fuel depot. Scott was the last member of the party to die and patriotically wrote in his diary: 'Had we lived I should have had a tale to tell of the hardiest endurance and courage of my companions which would have stirred the heart of every Englishman. These rough notes and our dead bodies must tell the tale…'

When Amundsen and Scott conquered the South Pole, Shackleton decided to attempt the first crossing of the Antarctic, a daunting 2,000 mile trip from the Weddell to the Ross Sea. The expedition, involving twenty-eight men, became a spectacular failure when their ship *Endurance* became trapped and crushed by ice. Hopelessly marooned, Shackleton ordered his men onto the ice and after four months drifting on their 'iceberg' they landed at Elephant Island in April 1916. Shackleton then realised that their only hope of survival was to reach the whaling stations on South Georgia Island, 800 miles away.

In one of the greatest small boat journeys ever made, he and five companions completed the crossing in seventeen days. To summon help from the whaling stations on the far side of the island, Shackleton and two of his men climbed the unsurveyed Alladyce Range in ten days and commandeered a Chilean steamer to rescue the three remaining members of the party on Elephant Island, finding them 'All safe. All well!'

Feted for his heroics in South America, Shackleton travelled to San Francisco before sailing to New Zealand, where a ship was provided to relieve the party stranded in the Ross Sea. Led by the indefatigable Shackleton, the rescuers arrived in January 1917 and discovered that all but three of the twenty-three men had survived the year-long ordeal. In a subsequent book, *South*, about the doomed venture that took place in the midst of the First World War, Shackleton dedicated it: 'To my comrades who fell in the white warfare of the south and on the red fields of France and Flanders'.

While embarking on his fourth polar expedition to explore 'all the oceanic and sub-Antarctic islands' in 1922, the intrepid Shackleton died from a heart attack on board his ship *Quest* at Grytviken, South Georgia Island, where he lies buried. The last words written in his diary shortly before his sudden death read: 'In the darkening twilight, I saw a lone star hover gem-like above the bay'.

Agatha Christie wrote a short mystery story, 'The Adventure of the Christmas Pudding' (1960) and, if ever a true-life adventure involving this festive treat occurred, it was in 1902 when Scott and Shackleton were jointly making their first attempt to reach the South Pole (an expedition obliquely referred to in the short-story collection *The Thirteen Problems* (1932), when a polar explorer writes an important letter before perishing during the plot of 'The Idol House of Astarte'). On Christmas Day, Shackleton conjured up a surprise to raise the morale of his fellow polar explorer, who recorded the joyous occasion:

> I had observed Shackleton ferreting about in his bundle, out of which he presently produced a spare sock. Stored away in that sock was a small round object about the size of a cricket ball, which when brought to light, proved to be a notable plum pudding. Another dive into his lucky bag and out came a crumpled piece of artificial holly. Heated in the cocoa, our plum pudding was soon steaming hot, and stood on the cooker-lid crowned with its decoration. Our Christmas Day had proved a delightful break in an otherwise uninterrupted spell of semi-starvation. Some days elapsed before its pleasing effects wore off.

16

BILLIE CARLETON

The Affair at the Victory Ball

Billie Carleton had a certain frail beauty of that perishable, moth-like substance that does not last long in the wear and tear of this rough-and-ready world.

Evening News

A collection of Agatha Christie short stories, which originally appeared in magazines between 1923 to 1926, was published as *The Underdog and Other Stories* (1951) and included 'The Affair at the Victory Ball', in which Hercule Poirot and Captain Hastings investigate a well-publicised society mystery where a young woman has been found dead of a cocaine overdose. With the addition of another death on the same night, where the drug victim's aristocratic fiancé is found stabbed to death, the mystery is based on the first great sex and drugs scandal of the twentieth century, in which the promising show-business career of actress, dancer and singer Billie Carleton came to a tragic end. A member of a fast-living set, the beautiful actress died from an overdose of cocaine. She was found dead in bed after an all-night party following the Victory Ball at the Royal Albert Hall to celebrate the end of the First World War in November 1918. Her Chinese drug suppliers became the target of hysterical press coverage about the growing threat of a 'yellow peril' in the Limehouse area of London. The case inspired several books, plays and films, notably Noël Coward's *The Vortex*, D.W. Griffiths's *Broken Blossoms*, based on a story by Thomas Burke, and Sax Rohmer's incredibly successful novels, adapted into over thirty films, about an evil empire in Limehouse controlled by 'Dr Fu Manchu – the yellow peril incarnate in one man'.

Billie Carleton.

Billie Carleton (1886–1918) was given leading roles in musical plays and revues produced by the top impresarios of the day, André Charlot and Charles B. Cochran, before she developed a serious drug habit that impeded her progress to becoming a star. During the run of *Watch Your Step* in 1914, Cochran was told that Carleton was being 'influenced by some undesirable people and was going to opium parties'.

The actress enjoyed a luxurious lifestyle, backed by three men in her life: 'Sugar daddy' John Marsh, twenty years her senior, whose wealth provided a permanent flat in Saville Row, Knightsbridge; physician Frederick Stuart, who managed her finances; and Bond Street costumier Reggie de Veulle, the man responsible for introducing her to drugs.

Arriving at the Victory Ball escorted by Dr Stuart, Carleton wore a daringly provocative dress made of transparent black georgette commissioned from de Veulle, who had asked heroin addict and actor Lionel Belcher to pass a silver box containing cocaine to the actress. Next day, Carleton's maid could not wake her mistress and called Dr Stuart, who administered an injection of strychnine and brandy in a vain attempt to revive the patient from the effects of 'cocaine poisoning'.

Lurid details of the late actress's lifestyle disclosed how Carleton and de Veulle held 'opium parties' and 'disgusting orgies' during which Ada Ping You, the Scottish wife of a Limehouse drug dealer, Lau Ping You, would arrive to cook the intoxicating concoction. The normally staid *Times* reported these activities in a headline article 'An Opium Circle. Chinaman's Wife Sent to Prison. High Priestess of Unholy Rites':

> After dinner the party… provided themselves with cushions and pillows, placed these on the floor, and sat themselves in a circle. The men divested themselves of their clothing and got into pyjamas, and the women into chiffon dresses… Miss Carleton arrived later at the flat from the theatre, and she, after disrobing, took her place in this circle of degenerates.

The trial of the drug dealers at the centre of the scandal resulted in Ada Ping You being sentenced to five months hard labour, although her husband escaped with just a £10 fine. In court it emerged that the married Reggie de Veulle had previously been involved in a homosexual blackmail case. However, contrary to the judge's direction, the jury acquitted him of the manslaughter of Billie Carleton. He admitted, however, to supplying the victim with cocaine and was sentenced to eight months imprisonment.

In 'The Affair at the Victory Ball', Agatha Christie's murderous drug peddlers are an English couple, a scenario that happily avoids the xenophobic approach to the true-life case employed by other authors; an unfortunate reflection of contemporary press coverage, typified by the *Evening News*. The fear of the evil influence of foreign men on the behaviour of innocent women drove them to issue a dire warning about the spectre of the opium den and the white slave trade, stating that it was the 'duty of every Englishman and Englishwoman to know the truth about the degradation of young white girls', published under the banner headline: 'White Girls Hypnotised by Yellow Men'.

STRANGER THAN FICTION

Following Agatha Christie's death, her final novel *Sleeping Murder* (1976) was published featuring the last case of Miss Marple, written during the Second World War and then kept in a vault. In the book a woman returns to her childhood home, where events trigger long-suppressed memories of the time when she saw the murdered body of her mother.

Amazingly, in 1979 real-life similarities with Christie's story occurred in North Carolina, where Annie Perry started having terrifying 'visions' of the time when she was aged ten and her father suddenly disappeared from the family farm in April 1944. Annie's flashbacks recalled how on Easter Sunday, she had seen her mother in the kitchen with the sink full of pots and pans in bloody water, the naked body of her father in an unused room and the noise of butchering sounds in the night. The week after her father's disappearance, when using the outside privy, she clearly remembered seeing his face floating in the water. After consulting a psychiatrist about these disturbing visions, she was advised to make a report to the police. They took the matter seriously and dug up the site of the old privy, where human remains were duly found.

Annie's mother, Winnie Cameron, had reported her husband missing and in due course obtained a divorce on grounds of desertion. When the gruesome discovery was made thirty-five years later, she shot herself, leaving a note confessing to the murder.

17

THE SINKING OF THE *LUSITANIA*

The Secret Adversary

The torpedoing of the Lusitania was a premeditated crime… This could only be done by vampires in human form.

Western Morning News

Agatha Christie introduced courting 'partners in crime' Tommy Beresford and Tuppence Crowley in *The Secret Adversary* (1922). The novel is not a murder mystery but a thriller, cleverly mixing fact with fiction. Set after the end of the First World War, the childhood friends meet up and, seeking excitement and gainful employment, they form a business called 'Young Adventurers'. After placing a newspaper advertisement offering to do anything and go anywhere, they are recruited by the Secret Service and become embroiled in the murky world of espionage, seeking the whereabouts of a young woman, Jane Finn, who, as she queued for a lifeboat, was handed highly sensitive wartime documents by an intelligence agent about to go down on a ship attacked by a U-boat, including a treaty that could still embarrass the government in peacetime. Tommy and Tuppence begin their investigation by tracking down surviving passengers to learn what they can of Jane Finn's fate in what was a true-life international incident, the sinking of the SS *Lusitania*.

In May 1915, the Cunard liner *Lusitania* set sail on her last voyage, with 1,257 passengers and 702 crew aboard. Travelling from New York to Liverpool, she was sunk by a U-boat eight miles off the coast of Ireland with the loss of

A recruiting poster produced in the wake of the tragedy.

1,198 lives. Too late, a lookout on the bow sounded the alarm through a megaphone, 'Torpedoes coming on the starboard side!' The torpedo struck the *Lusitania* under the bridge and triggered a second explosion of a deadly cargo onboard the ship. A shocked survivor recalled, 'It sounded like a million-ton hammer hitting a steam boiler a hundred feet high'.

The barbarism of an attack on an unarmed and unescorted passenger ship without warning brought widespread condemnation, summed up by the following comment in the press: 'Fifteen hundred non-combatants murdered in cold-blood… has produced a feeling of horror and abhorrence which cannot, and should not, be confined to impotent fury'. However, it was not generally known at the time that apart from passengers, the liner was also carrying munitions, arguably making it a legitimate military target. Only a week earlier, the German embassy had warned US citizens of the dangers of travelling on a published list of vessels that included the *Lusitania*. When news of the loss broke in England, rioters took to the streets and attacked shops with German-sounding names in cities across the country, including London, Manchester and Liverpool. Mobs then targeted other minority groups, including Jewish and Chinese communities, forcing the government to send in troops to restore order and the introduction of a policy to intern 'enemy aliens' for the duration of the war.

Although outraged, there was no comparable violent reaction in the USA, despite the fact that 128 US citizens had drowned in the atrocity. A year later Woodrow Wilson was elected President on a peace platform, naïvely asserting that 'there is such a thing as a nation being so right that it does not need to convince others by force that it is right'. Continuing to pursue a policy of neutrality in spite of continued provocation, he delivered his famous 'Peace without Victory' speech in January 1917. However, at the end of that same month, Germany dropped any pretence that that it would show any restraint towards 'neutral shipping' – officially making any merchant vessel a target for U-boats – when a message from the German Foreign Minister, Dr Arthur Zimmerman, was intercepted. It revealed plans to recommence unrestricted submarine warfare and proposed an alliance between Germany and Mexico if America entered the war, with a promise that the disputed ownership of the lands of Texas and Arizona would be resolved by handing them back to Mexico. When this news was leaked by British intelligence, isolationist feelings dissolved and had the desired effect for the cause of the Allies. Fury ensued in the US following the sinking of three cargo vessels in March 1917, forcing Wilson to abandon his neutral stance. American forces were soon on their way to Europe after the President reluctantly approached Congress to endorse a declaration of war on Germany. He won their full support with an eloquent address, accepting that, 'The world must be made safe for democracy'.

18

LAWRENCE OF ARABIA

They Came to Baghdad

Fakir Carmichael is modelled on soldier, scholar and Arabist T.E. Lawrence.

The Agatha Christie Collection No. 42, *They Came to Baghdad*

Agatha Christie's light-hearted thriller *They Came to Baghdad* (1951) features a multilingual member of British intelligence, Henry 'Fakir' Carmichael, a character based on the real-life persona of the enigmatic T.E. Lawrence (1888-1935). The real-life hero turned down a recommendation for the Victoria Cross and the offer of a knighthood for his role as guerrilla leader of the Arab Revolt against Germany's allies, the Turks, during the First World War. The 'Uncrowned King of the Desert' was a brilliant scholar, philosopher, archaeologist, linguist, author, diplomat and statesman who shunned fame and fortune to become an aircraft mechanic in what was a forlorn attempt to escape the charismatic image he had engendered as the world-renowned 'Lawrence of Arabia'.

One of Lawrence's ancestors was the cousin of Sir Walter Raleigh, a connection of which he was extremely proud. Therefore, it was fitting that in February 1929 Lawrence journeyed to the county of Raleigh's birth to be stationed at RAF Mountbatten, Plymouth. In an effort to escape undue attention he had assumed the alias 'Shaw', in honour of one of his great friends, Irish playwright George Bernard Shaw, who introduced him to the vivacious Lady Nancy Astor. She was one of the most glamorous figures of the interwar period and had the distinction of being the first female to enter Parliament after women had been given their long overdue right to vote in 1918.

T.E. Lawrence.

She succeeded her husband, Waldorf, as member for Plymouth Sutton when he moved to the Lords, and continued to serve the city until she retired from politics in 1945.

Lawrence was asexual and a cynical woman-hater, but became an ardent admirer of American-born Nancy and her incredible zest for life. She was the only female allowed to ride pillion on his motorbike. The pair would often shoot off on his powerful 1,000cc Brough Superior for a high-speed ride around the city and boasted of reaching speeds of 90mph along Plymouth Embankment. In October 1930, Lawrence wrote to tell Nancy how he had overtaken a Bentley sports car 'which only did 88' on Salisbury Plain: 'I wished I had had a peeress or two on my flapper bracket'.

Lawrence called his bike Boanerges (meaning 'Sons of Thunder', the name which Jesus gave to two of his disciples, James and John), but his love of speed was to cause his tragic death shortly after his discharge from the RAF in March 1935. Taking up residence at Cloud's Hill, a rented cottage in Dorset, he found it difficult to face an uncertain future and friends became concerned as he had attempted suicide in the past. He wrote to Nancy:

I am so tired that it feels like heaven drawing near: only there are people who whisper that heaven will bore me. When they tell me that I almost wish I were dead for I have done everything in life except rest, and if rest is to prove no refuge, then what is left?

Lady Astor tried to cheer Lawrence with the promise of a forthcoming government post and invited him to her country house in Buckinghamshire: 'I believe... you will be asked to help reorganise the Defence Forces. If you will come to Cliveden, the last Saturday in May... you will never regret it'.

Britain needed men of Lawrence's calibre in preparing to counter the growing threat posed by Germany. On the 13 May Lawrence received a letter from the award-winning author of *Tarka the Otter*, Henry Williamson, based in Georgeham, North Devon, proposing a meeting at Cloud's Hill to discuss the possibility of Lawrence holding talks with Adolf Hitler to try and secure a lasting peace in Europe. Williamson was a member of Oswald Mosely's British Union of Fascists and fervent admirer of the Fuhrer's achievements. His collected novels, *The Flax of Dream*, contained the following dedication: 'I salute the great man across the Rhine whose life symbol is a happy child'.

Lawrence agreed to receive Williamson and rode to the Post Office to send a telegram with the following directions: 'Lunch Tuesday will find cottage one mile north of Bovington Camp SHAW'.

On his way back home he swerved his motorcycle to avoid two errand boys on bicycles, crashed and flew over the handlebars, receiving severe head injuries. Lawrence was taken to Bovington Military Hospital but never recovered consciousness and died six days later. The ghost of Lawrence wearing flowing, long Arab robes was soon spotted riding a motorbike by Cloud's Hill. Chillingly, a year before his death, Lawrence had prophesised his demise in a letter to motorbike manufacturer George Brough: 'It looks as though I might yet break my neck on a Brough Superior'.

Agatha Christie's fictional hero, Fakir Carmichael, is killed while trying to relay plans to his supervisor about a secret weapon; likewise, following Lawrence's death, rumours circulated that he had been murdered by foreign agents. Conversely, another story circulated that his death had been faked by the Secret Service to allow him to undertake espionage in the Middle East. Supporters of this theory believe he died in Morocco in 1968. In keeping with similar tales about heroic figures, including Francis Drake, Horatio Nelson and Lord Kitchener, there is also a legend that Lawrence has merely withdrawn into an Arthurian limbo from which he will emerge to save an imperilled nation.

19

EDEN PHILLPOTTS

Peril at End House

Eden Phillpotts was an odd-looking man, with a face more like a faun's than an ordinary human being's.

Agatha Christie (*An Autobiography*, 1977)

In *Peril at End House* (1932), Poirot and Hastings go to the aid of a young woman in danger at an eerie mansion, End House, whilst holidaying at the Majestic Hotel, St Loo. The properties are recognisable as Rock End and the Imperial Hotel in Torquay and Agatha Christie dedicated the mystery novel to one of the town's most famous former residents, prolific author Eden Phillpotts, in gratitude 'for his friendship and the encouragement he gave me many years ago'.

Born in India, the son of an Army officer who died while he was an infant, Eden Phillpotts (1862-1960) was raised and educated in Plymouth, then for ten years worked for an insurance company in London before he successfully turned to writing for a living after failing in his ambition to become an actor. For half a century Phillpotts produced an average of four major works a year, covering novels, poems, plays, short stories and even detective stories, using the pseudonym Harrington Hext. However, he is best remembered as the 'Hardy of Devon' for a celebrated cycle of eighteen novels based on Dartmoor locations. Most notable was *Widecombe Fair* (1913), which he adapted into a play, *The Farmer's Wife*, that was later directed for the silent screen by Alfred Hitchcock. From 1899-1929, Phillpotts made his home at Eltham, Torquay, where he became good friends with his neighbours, the Miller family. When Agatha was aged nineteen, she wrote a novel based in

Above and below: The Imperial Hotel, which featured prominently in the novel *Peril at End House*.

Cairo called *Snow in the Desert* and approached Phillpotts for advice. He was sufficiently impressed to arrange a meeting for her with his London literary agent, Hughes Massie, who considered the manuscript for a few months before deciding he would not be able to place it with a publisher.

Phillpotts nurtured another talented writer in his own household, his daughter Adelaide Eden Phillpotts (1896-1993), who grew to admire Agatha Miller while they were attending dance classes together:

> Of all the children I recall only a flaxen-haired beauty of twelve called Agatha – later Agatha Christie – wearing a blue silk accordion-pleated dress, who danced better that anyone else and was prettier. She lived near us but we did not see much of her until she grew up. One side of the saloon held a large mirror and I recollect on my sixth birthday standing in front of it and noticing my face for the first time. Then I caught a sight of Agatha's reflection: she was a thousand times nicer and cleverer than me. But I never envied anyone.

However, at this same young stage of her life Adelaide was harbouring a dark secret, as her innocence was in peril at Eltham. The young girl had become sexually attractive to her own father and it was many years before she could bring herself to reveal the sordid nature of their incestuous relationship:

> He had begun deeply to love me. I think he looked on me as an extension of himself, for he would take me into his bed and fondle me, compare my limbs with his and say 'Look! Your hands and feet are just like small editions of mine. You are so like me. And you going to be a writer too'. He kissed me all over and said: 'You must never marry!' At six or seven that meant nothing to me. Yet I did not forget those words, which all through my youth and afterwards were repeated. I loved him too but only as a father, and for fear of hurting him I let him do whatever he liked.

When Adelaide was older, she was made aware of her father's infidelities by her mother, who explained that he had always needed other women in his life, while he himself justified his licentious lifestyle to his daughter by stating his belief that 'all artists, especially writers of fiction and drama, must gather as much knowledge as possible about the opposite sex'.

Adelaide was a versatile writer, producing a total of forty-two major works, including four written in corroboration with her father. Unsurprisingly given the nature of her upbringing and personal experience, a core group of seven novels, including *A Marriage* (1928) and *The Gallant Heart* (1939), do not feature heroes, but heroines who commonly share a deep distrust of men. Forever fearful of her father's cruel hold over her, she did not find the courage

Eden Phillpotts.

to break free from his evil spell until the age of fifty-five, when she fell in 'love at first sight' with a divorced American bookseller, Richard Ross. In 1951, the couple were married after a six-month courtship despite the vehement objections of Eden Phillpotts, whom Adelaide deemed to have 'no power over love'. During his mid-sixties in 1929, the veteran author had married a young cousin with whom he began an affair while his first wife was dying of cancer, but in his late-eighties still could not accept his daughter's right to happiness with another man. He obstinately refused to meet the groom and never spoke to his daughter again, presumably because she had gone against his express wish to 'love him best until the end'.

The blameless victim of sexual abuse was tormented by the estrangement from her father, a situation that continued to cast 'a shadow on my joys, a tangle in my golden threads, a satin on my sunrise, some regret, fear, remorse, guilt, or pity, to mar the bliss'.

Poignantly, Eden Phillpotts's extreme possessiveness and jealousy also ruined his loyal and loving daughter's chance to fulfil her greatest desire – to have a child. Two days after Agatha Christie gave birth to her daughter Rosalind in 1919, Adelaide paid a visit to see the mother and child at Ashfield. She felt 'an indescribable thrill' as she held the newborn infant, hopefully, though forlornly, telling herself, 'You must have as many of these as possible'.

20

CHARLES LINDBERGH

Murder on the Orient Express

The kidnapping and murder of the Lindbergh baby is a never-to-be-forgotten case.

President Herbert Hoover

Central to the plot of the mystery novel *Murder on the Orient Express* (1934) is the kidnapping and murder of a child, for which Agatha Christie drew inspiration from the contemporary publicity surrounding the infamous real-life tragedy that befell the family of a famous aviator. It sparked the world's greatest manhunt for the abductor of 'Baby Lindbergh'.

In 1927 American Charles Lindbergh (1902–1974), nicknamed 'The Lone Eagle', was feted as a national hero when he made the first ever non-stop solo transatlantic flight from New York to Paris in a single-engine aeroplane, *The Spirit of St Louis*. Sadly, he made international headlines again five years later when his twenty-one-month-old son, Charles Augustus Lindbergh Jr, was kidnapped from his bedroom in Hopewell, New Jersey, in March 1932. At the luxurious home, complete with an English butler, the perpetrator left behind a ransom note demanding $50,000 for the baby's safe return. After protracted negotiation, intermediary Dr Condon journeyed to the Bronx and handed the ransom money over a cemetery wall to someone calling himself 'John'. The anxious father was then directed to the Massachusetts coast, assured that his son was safe and sound on a boat. This proved to be a cruel hoax, for the distraught airman spent days flying over the area without locating a boat or his child. The ordeal of Lindbergh and his wife Anne continued until the baby's body was found in a shallow grave in a wood four miles from

A souvenir of Lindbergh's
historic flight.

their home. Death had been caused by a massive fracture of the skull from a
blow delivered soon after he had been taken. A nationwide hunt for the killer
was launched and the serial numbers of the banknotes used to pay the ransom
were printed in newspapers across the country. It was to be over two years
before one turned up when a German-born carpenter with a history of petty
crime bought some petrol at a filling station in the Bronx in September 1934.

Illegal immigrant Bruno 'Richard' Hauptmann was arrested after the
sharp-eyed filling-station attendant furnished the police with his car regis-
tration number and, despite protesting his innocence, the evidence against
the accused was compelling. The ransom note contained spelling errors
that suggested the writer was German, whilst a search of the suspect's house
recovered $14,000 of the original ransom money found hidden in the garage.
Also, a wooden floorboard missing from the attic had been used to make
the homemade ladder used in the kidnapping and Dr Condon's telephone

number was found written on a piece of paper. Hauptmann was sentenced to death in February 1935 and, after being granted three postponements, went to the electric chair fifteen months later. In the words of one reporter who witnessed the execution, the murderer paid the 'supreme penalty' for his heinous crime 'without uttering a word and with a wistful smile on his pallid face'. Revulsion at Hauptmann's crime of killing the baby affectionately known as 'The Little Eagle' had been felt by even hardened criminals, including Chicago gangster Al Capone, the instigator of the infamous St Valentine's Day Massacre in 1929. At the time of the kidnapping, Capone offered a $10,000 reward and volunteered his services to locate the missing baby. However, 'Scarface' was unable to obtain the cooperation of the government to release him from San Francisco's Alcatraz where he was serving a ten-year jail sentence, not for any of his prohibition rackets or violent crimes, but for failing to submit tax returns to Uncle Sam!

Curiously, Agatha Christie's *Murder on the Orient Express* came to the forefront in a different context when the English Riviera became the first urban area to be granted Geopark status in 2007. Nick Powe, Managing Director of the prehistoric Kents Cavern, which featured as Hemsley Cavern in *The Man in the Brown Suit* (1924), welcomed the prestigious award recognising the area's 'fabulous wildlife, marine biology, sea grasses, dolphins, archaeological and geological heritage'. It would also enable the promotion of many more of Torbay's assets, 'including links to the works of... Agatha Christie', whose keen interest in archaeology had brought about her meeting with second husband Max Mallowan. Two of the Geopark's gateway sites, Torquay Museum and Torre Abbey, have permanent exhibitions celebrating Agatha Christie's life. Furthermore, 'The Queen of Crime' has inspired a palaeontology theory developed by American Douglas Erwin, the world's leading expert on the global catastrophe that occurred at the end of the Permian period some 250 million years ago when 90 per cent of all life on Earth became extinct. His books on the subject, described as 'whodunnits for the ages', are written from the perspective of a forensic scientist trying to piece together minute clues to determine the many possible causes of death that include asteroid impact, huge volcanic eruptions or the oceans losing their oxygen content. Unfolding as a sort of geological mystery story, Erwin describes a final possibility as the 'Murder on the Orient Express' scenario which, like fictional detective Hercule Poirot of the novel, proposes that the murder was committed by all the suspects.

STRANGER THAN FICTION

In September 1976 a prosecutor told a court how a girl from the Isle of Wight, aged fifteen, attempted to kill her parents after becoming 'immersed in the detective fiction of Agatha Christie'.

The girl had been adopted at the age of six and was well treated by her devoted parents, who were devastated to hear her plead guilty to deliberately damaging their car and committing arson with intent to endanger life. After failing to cause an accident by cutting what she believed was the brake line on the family car, the accused set the vehicle alight in the integrated garage. The fire spread to the house, where her parents were watching television. They escaped from the inferno after making a desperate attempt to reach their daughter's room where they believed she was trapped. However, the arsonist was admiring her handiwork from the top of a nearby cliff and later admitted, 'I wanted to kill Mum and Dad. They expected too much of me. They expected me to be a goody-goody all the time. I wanted to show them I was not. I wanted them dead'.

Treated sympathetically by the judge, who ordered her detention until she received treatment that would make her fit 'to be at large in the world again', the defence counsel added, 'It is very difficult in dealing with a person with intense imagination to discover where play acting ends and reality begins'.

21

FRANK VOSPER

Love From A Stranger

Vosper… drowned after falling from a transatlantic liner and his death was only ruled as an accident after much media speculation, involving alleged sexual she-nanigans aboard the ship. Sounds as though the bizarre and tragic episode could have provided the raw material for a fictional mystery.

Crime writer Martin Edwards

Agatha Christie granted her permission for 'Philomel Cottage', from the short story collection *The Listerdale Mystery* (1934), to be adapted for the stage. It was renamed *Love From a Stranger* by the dramatist, who subsequently became the focus of a real-life mystery when he either fell or jumped to his death from the porthole of an ocean liner off the coast of Devon.

The play was written by actor, producer and playwright Frank Vosper (1899-1937), then at the height of his fame having established himself as one of the most versatile members of the theatrical and film world. During the interwar years he established himself as a thespian of distinction with his portrayal of Henry VIII in *The Rose Without a Thorn*, and a successful dramatist with the comedy *No Funny Business* and crime story *Murder on the Second Floor*. Having made his screen debut in 1926, he appeared in many films, tending to be typecast as an urbane villain – notably in Alfred Hitchcock's first version of *The Man Who Knew Too Much* (1934).

In 1936, *Love From A Stranger* opened at the New Theatre, London, with Frank Vosper starring in a plot that centres on a young woman's fear of her husband's past and the threat posed to her life. The success of the play resulted

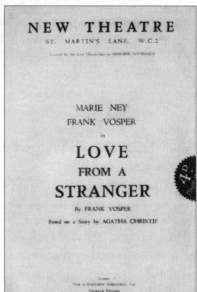

NEW THEATRE
ST. MARTIN'S LANE. W.C.2

MARIE NEY
FRANK VOSPER
in
LOVE
FROM A
STRANGER
By FRANK VOSPER
Based on a Story by AGATHA CHRISTIE

Frank Vosper.   Programme of the theatre play.

in the first British film adaptation of a work by Agatha Christie. Starring Basil Rathbone, who would find lasting fame in the role of Sherlock Homes, and featuring a young Joan Hickson, later endorsed by Agatha Christie as the perfect choice to play Miss Marple, the screen version was released in 1937. Earlier that year, Vosper, accompanied by his close friend Peter Willes, holidayed in Jamaica and New York. Travelling back to England on the liner SS *Paris*, tragedy struck at an end of voyage party shortly before the ship was due to dock at Plymouth.

In the early hours of the morning on 6 March 1937, the reigning Miss Europe, Muriel Oxford, who had been visiting America for screen tests with a film studio, sought an introduction and was invited for drinks in the cabin shared by Frank Vosper and Peter Willes. At 2.45 a.m., passengers summoned a steward to interrupt the party and complain about the noise being made by the threesome who were quaffing champagne, resulting in the beauty queen taking the men to her stateroom where another large bottle of champagne was opened. Twenty minutes later, a man was heard to call out, 'If you don't marry me, I will jump overboard!' Minutes later, two of the revellers realised that while they had been sitting together and chatting, their fellow partygoer Frank Vosper had disappeared from the room – but had not left by the door. The alarm was raised but the captain refused to look for a 'man overboard' as he did not consider it possible for someone to slip and fall out of the porthole, but a search of the ship failed to find the missing person and the drowned body of the actor was eventually washed up at Eastbourne sixteen days later. In a statement to the press, Peter Willes clarified that it was he who had jokingly suggested 'marriage' and 'jumping overboard', and that his friend must have been trying to discreetly leave the party so as not appear rude. In his opinion, the actor's poor eyesight may have led him to believe that he could alight on the deck via the porthole. At the subsequent inquest, the coroner summarised that there was no question of an accident in the ordinary sense of a man climbing on to the ledge and falling through the window. Therefore, the only question that remained to answer was why had Frank Vosper leapt through the window? Was it with the intention of ending it all, or under the misapprehension that there was a deck on which he could land? If it was a case of suicide, then it must have been on a very sudden impulse, for there was no obvious reason to imply that the actor was considering taking his own life. If it was purely an accident, then the victim must have been attempting to leave unnoticed by the window to ensure he would not spoil the party that his 'merry' companions Mr Willes and Miss Oxford were so obviously enjoying.

Faced with a lack of concrete evidence, the jury returned an 'open verdict', although media sexual innuendo about what may have transpired between the two men and the actress prompted her to sue the proprietors of the *Daily Mirror* and the *Daily Mail* for articles 'capable of casting imputations on Miss Oxford's morality'. There was speculation that Vosper was upset that Muriel Oxford preferred Peter Willes's company to his, although with no Hercule Poirot on the case, there was a twist to the love triangle evidently not considered during the investigation. Due to the veil of secrecy surrounding homosexual activity, which was then illegal, Vosper may well have taken his own life, not out of longing for a beautiful woman, but in a fit of jealous rage at witnessing the sight of his gay partner, Peter Willes, cavorting with the would-be starlet. In theatre circles Vosper was well known to be homosexual, and his play *The Green Bay Tree* was popular with those in the know, for it obliquely depicted a gay aristocrat who picks up a working-class boy and models him in his own image. Frank Vosper and Peter Willes's relationship may well have held the key to the mysterious events of that fateful night on the liner, an aspect of the case that was summarised by the 1973 winner of the Nobel Prize for Literature, Patrick White. In his autobiography *Flaws in the Glass* (1981), the gay author and playwright remarked that it was commonly believed at the time of the tragedy that Vosper had 'thrown himself off a liner after finding his male lover flirting with a beauty queen'.

22

SIR CHRISTOPHER LEE

Murder Is Easy

John Lee the Butler is now sent for trial, committed for murder there is no denial,
Whether he done it, it is hard to say, it will be proved on some future day.

Broadsheet ballad (1884)

Distinguished actor Christopher Lee (b. 1922) was awarded a knighthood in 2009 in recognition of a long screen career, which included roles in the James Bond film *The Man With the Golden Gun* and the acclaimed adaptation of Tolkein's *Lord of the Rings* trilogy. During the 1990s, Lee narrated a number of audiobooks from the works of Agatha Christie – *Hound of Death*, *Witness For the Prosecution* and *The Call of Wings* – and was also heard, but not seen, as the uncredited voice of the mysterious host, Mr U.N. Owen, who records a message accusing his guests and servants of past crimes when they assemble on a remote island in the film *Ten Little Indians* (1965).

As an RAF pilot during the Second World War, Christopher Lee spent some time on the English Riviera stationed at an Initial Training Wing in Paignton. The recruits frequented the pubs in the nearby Babbacombe area of Torquay and learnt about 'The Man They Could Not Hang', the story of a local villain called John Lee who notoriously survived three attempts to execute him for murder. Predictably, the future star of Hammer horror films soon had to endure being called 'Lee of Babbacombe' by his colleagues. He later recalled in his autobiography, 'It became a constant joke among my mates that I wasn't to be provoked or trifled with, because I was one of the undead who cheat the gallows'.

FINDING THE BODY OF MISS KEYSE

THE BABBICOMBE MURDER- SHOCKING SCENES ON THE SCAFFOLD

His infamous namesake, John 'Babbacombe' Lee, had been arrested on purely circumstantial evidence in November 1884, charged with the gruesome murder of his elderly employer, Emma Keyse, at her home The Glen on Babbacombe Beach. Robbery had not been a committed and there was no sign of a forced entry, so therefore suspicion fell upon the only male among the four servants present in the house – John Lee.

Tried at Exeter Castle in February 1885, he was sentenced to hang. However, he incredibly escaped execution when the trapdoors of the scaffold mysteriously failed to open on three occasions when the prisoner stepped onto the platform, fuelling the legend of 'The Man They Could Not Hang'. Mortified officials abandoned the execution and the death penalty was commuted to life imprisonment following the intervention of Queen Victoria, who sent the following telegram to the Home Secretary: 'I am horrified at the disgraceful scenes at Exeter at Lee's execution. Surely Lee cannot be executed. It would be too cruel. Imprisonment for life seems the only alternative'. The Home Secretary concurred and told a packed House of Commons: 'It would shock the feelings of everyone if a man twice had to pay the pangs of imminent death'.

Although an official report concluded that the scaffold had failed due to a simple mechanical fault, the findings were not made public and many people believed God had acted to save an innocent man. In stark contrast to the prosecution's portrayal of a depraved lunatic capable of smashing an old lady's head with an axe, then slashing her throat with a knife before setting fire to the lifeless body, in passing the sentence of death the judge remarked how calm the demeanour of the accused had been throughout the trial. The prisoner leaned forward in the dock and replied firmly, 'The reason why I am so calm is that I trust in the Lord, and He knows I am innocent'. In the days leading up to the date of execution, Lee read the Bible prodigiously and intimated to the prison chaplain that the real culprit was the lover of his half-sister, Elizabeth Harris, who was cook at The Glen and expecting a child, which was later delivered in the workhouse. Following his reprieve, Lee announced his belief that he had been saved by divine intervention and on the morning of the execution told two prison guards that he had dreamt that 'Three times the bolt was drawn, and three times the bolt failed to act'.

John Lee fully expected to be released after serving twenty years imprisonment, which was the usual period served by reprieved murderers. He was not informed that as a bungle on the scaffold had brought about his survival, not the merits of his case, the Home Secretary had recommended that the prisoner should remain in confinement for the remainder of his natural life. When press rumours of Lee's imminent release did not materialise early in 1905, the prisoner's mother engaged the services of Newton Abbot solicitor

Katherine and Herbert Rowse
Armstrong.

Herbert Rowse Armstrong to gain justice for her son. Acting on her behalf, Armstrong wrote to enlist the support of local MP Harry Eve: 'I am quite aware that there is no statutory definition or power to diminish a life sentence, but the Home Office regulations do constantly allow of its reduction to 20 years and often less e.g. Mrs. Maybrick, as to almost nullify the effect'.

The writer of this letter little realised that fifteen years later, he, like the aforementioned Florence Maybrick, would deny charges of poisoning a spouse and be condemned to stand on the scaffold. The difference was that there would be no reprieve for Armstrong, who would go down in the annals of British criminal history as the only solicitor ever to be hanged for murder.

A year after representing John Lee, Armstrong married and set up a law practice in the Welsh border town of Hay-on-Wye. After serving as a major in the Territorial Army during the First World War, he was demobbed in 1919 and his neglected business soon ran into financial difficulties. As his law practice floundered, he purchased arsenic, ostensibly to treat a patch of dandelions on his lawn, but administered it to his wife Katherine. She passed away in 1921 shortly after changing her will, leaving everything to her husband. Natural causes were accepted as the cause of death, but suspicions were aroused when the major attempted to poison a business rival and the exhumation of his wife's body revealed that deadly levels of arsenic had caused her demise. The Armstrong case is recalled by characters in the Christie novels *After the Funeral* and *Sleeping Murder*, whilst in *Murder Is Easy* (1939) Major Horton, whose wife dies of 'gastritis', is clearly based on the real-life murderer dubbed 'The Dandelion Killer'.

During Agatha's childhood, she enjoyed family picnics at the infamous crime scene on Babbacombe Beach. She cannot have failed to learn more about the sensational story when John Lee gained his release in 1907 and published his autobiography serialised in a national newspaper – proclaiming that it was not the butler 'whodunnit'.

23

DENNIS O'NEILL

The Mousetrap

The Mousetrap is to the West End Theatre what the ravens are to the Tower of London. Its disappearance could impoverish us.

The Financial Times

Agatha Christie's murder mystery *The Mousetrap* originated as a thirty-minute radio play entitled *Three Blind Mice*, the nursery rhyme that is the theme song of a murderer who plans to kill three victims. The drama was commissioned by the BBC at the request of Queen Mary after the corporation enquired what she would like to hear for her eightieth birthday in 1947. Her Royal Highness replied that she would like nothing better than to listen to a play by Agatha Christie, and the delighted author set about creating a classic 'who-dunnit' – that would later develop into a theatrical tour de force and become the world's longest running play – by choosing a plot based on a real-life case.

Two years earlier, Agatha had been deeply moved by a horrific case result-ing in the brutal death of a young boy, Dennis O'Neill, at Bank Farm, near Minsterley, Shropshire. Dennis and his younger brother Terrence had been maltreated by their foster parents, Reginald and Esther Gough. Terrence O'Neill testified that the boys were usually fed drinks of tea and only three slices of bread and butter each per day. They stole whatever they could from the pantry to supplement their diet and would even suck milk from the teats of the farm cows. Every night both boys were routinely given a severe thrashing with a stick on their hands and legs, sometimes receiving up to 100 blows each before the sadistic farmer made them say their prayers. On 19 March 1945,

The Mousetrap now showing at St Martin's Theatre.

the jury deliberated for only twenty minutes before finding that the twelve-year-old had been beaten to death after his tormentor tied him to a bench in the kitchen of his farmhouse as punishment for eating a swede. Reginald Gough was convicted of manslaughter and sentenced to six years in prison, while Esther Gough, who had been terrified for her own safety at the hands of her husband, was jailed for six months on charges of neglect.

Agatha wondered how the trauma of such a childhood would affect a survivor in later life and developed the character of a similarly abused child whose ordeal leads him to grow up seeking revenge. When the play was expanded into *The Mousetrap* and opened at London's Ambassadors Theatre on 25 November 1952, the author thought that it might run for six months at most; a view shared by the editor of the 1953 *Theatre Annual*, who gallantly chose not to disclose the identity of the killer:

> Suffice to say the interest is held and everyone appears more or less guilty until the most unlikely character in the cast is caught red-handed when about to commit the third murder. In case the play is still running when this appears in print we forebear to mention the name!

During the first 700 performances of the phenomenal run, the pivotal role of Detective Sergeant Trotter, the policemen who arrives at a snowbound guesthouse to warn the visitors that there is a killer amongst them, was played by Richard Attenborough. Tragically, his long and distinguished career was not matched by the talented actor who immediately succeeded him in the part: Patric Doonan. He took over the role in August 1954 before leaving three years later to appear in *All Kinds of Men*, a new American play at the Arts Theatre by Alex Samuels. However, his next venture at the St Martin's Theatre in February 1958, appearing in Anthony Pelissiere's drama *Roseland*, proved disastrous and closed after only three nights as the implausible plot brought howls of derision from the audience. Although the reviewer from *The Times* was full of praise for his performance, writing: 'Patric Doonan is excellent as the business-like ex-convict', a month later the body of the thirty-one-year-old was found in a gas-filled room at his home in Chelsea. Letters found at the scene indicated that he intended to take his own life and at the subsequent inquest, the coroner found that suicide was the cause of death. Despite becoming recently engaged to actress Ann Firbank, the dead man's brother, actor Tony Doonan, told the coroner that Patric had become rather depressed as 'his show had collapsed on him'. The actor's name lives on in a song by rock singer Morrissey, 'Now My Heart is Full'.

In March 1959, the cast from the Ambassadors Theatre found themselves involved at the scene of a real investigation. Using sets built by the prisoners, they agreed to put on a special Sunday performance of *The Mousetrap* for 300 inmates at Wormwood Scrubs, but as the play was reaching its thrilling climax in the final act, the alarm was sounded when warders suddenly discovered that two members of the captive audience were missing. A hue and cry ensued when it was realised that David Gooding and John Meyers, both serving three-year sentences for theft, had slipped away from the show unnoticed. The convicts made good their escape and were on the run for several weeks before they were recaptured.

24

KLAUS FUCHS AND BRUNO PONTECORVO

Destination Unknown

Agatha Christie writes animated algebra.

Francis Wyndham (The *Sunday Times*, 1966)

Agatha Christie's novel *Destination Unknown* (1954) concerns the mysterious disappearance of several important scientists. The story is set against the background of the Cold War between the leading international powers, and was directly inspired by the true-life defection of top physicists Klaus Fuchs and Bruno Pontecorvo, who betrayed the West by passing atomic secrets to Communist Russia.

German Klaus Fuchs (1911–1988) despised the Hitler regime and moved to Britain to complete his education in the 1930s. Having a brilliant mind for physics and maths, he obtained his PhD in Bristol and his ScD in Edinburgh. However, the fact that he was a German and a member of the Communist Party led to his detention at the outset of the Second World War and he was sent to an internment camp in Canada. Although he was subsequently released when agents accepted that his anti-Nazi sentiments were genuine, and then took up the offer of British citizenship and secured an important job working on scientific projects for the war effort, Fuchs still felt aggrieved at the treatment he had received. When approached by a Russian agent, he agreed to pass on any scientific secrets he learned to the Soviet Union. He believed that because the Russians were Allies fighting the Nazis, they had the

Klaus Fuchs.

moral right to know what America and Great Britain were doing to develop the atomic bomb.

In 1944, Fuchs joined the staff working on atomic energy at Columbia University in New York City. Once a week, he walked to a street corner in downtown Manhattan and handed over reams of handwritten notes detailing the ongoing research to Russian-born immigrant Harry Gold. Transferred to Los Alamos, New Mexico, Fuchs worked on the actual construction of the bomb and the world learned of the lethal discovery when Hiroshima and Nagasaki were totally destroyed in 1945. When news of the first blast reached Los Alamos, the team engaged on the project decided to celebrate their success that so dramatically brought about the end of the war with Japan. Fuchs volunteered to drive into Santa Fe and buy some liquor and met Harry Gold in a bar, where he handed over complete instructions on how to build the bomb and detonate it. The traitor returned to England and joined the staff of the atomic research centre at Harwell in 1946 – the same year that Winston Churchill identified the existence of the 'Iron Curtain'. Fuchs realised that his actions may have been naïve and dropped all contact with the Soviets. However, his past crimes caught up with him in January 1950 when an associate of Harry Gold bragged about the recruitment of a top British scientist and Fuchs soon became the prime suspect. During interrogation the physicist admitted his involvement and his statements led to the arrest of his handler Gold, who in turn revealed the full extent of the espionage and the role of laboratory worker David Greengrass. He had passed on information to his relatives, Soviet couriers Julius and Ethel Rosenberg, the American husband and wife team who were subsequently executed for their part in the spy ring.

Tried and sentenced to fourteen years imprisonment, Fuchs was released after serving nine years in Wormwood Scrubs and immediately travelled to East Germany, where the Soviets placed him in charge of nuclear research at Dresden – a reward for presenting them with the world's most powerful weapon free of charge.

Eight months after the disappearance of Klaus Fuchs, another brilliant scientist, Bruno Pontecorvo (1913-1993), failed to return to England after going on holiday with his family. Born in Pisa, the brother of film director Gillo Pontecorvo and geneticist Guido Pontecorvo, the physicist had left Italy in the 1930s to avoid the Fascist regime's discrimination against his Jewish faith. He lived in Paris until the Nazis entered the city in the Second World War, then worked in America until he was invited to contribute to the British atomic bomb project at Harwell in 1947. However, in August 1951, he abruptly abandoned his holiday in Rome and, accompanied by his wife and three children, boarded a plane for Stockholm without informing friends or relatives. Fears for his motives grew when a passenger on the flight revealed that five-year-old Antonio Pontecorvo had told him that the family were going to Russia. Unbeknown to the security services, Soviet agents had helped the Pontecorvos to enter the USSR from Finland. Confirmation of this outcome was not forthcoming until 1955, when Pontecorvo held a news conference in Moscow declaring that he had been granted refuge in the Soviet Union where he was involved in nuclear research for peaceful purposes and had left the West because, in his view, it was intent (like the megalomaniac in Agatha Christie's novel) on 'new war using atomic and nuclear weapons as means for achieving world domination'.

In Christie's political thriller *Passenger to Frankfurt* (1970) two characters discuss the most sensational spy scandal of the post-war period when Guy Burgess and Donald Maclean escaped arrest for their treachery by seeking sanctuary in the Soviet Union. With a theatrical flourish, the partners in crime fled the country on a ferry from Southampton to France en route to Moscow in May 1951, with Maclean dressed in drag and posing as Burgess's wife. Guy Burgess, a native of Devonport who had undergone service training at the Britannia Royal Naval College on the River Dart near Greenway, was fully conversant with the novels of Agatha Christie and playfully fooled the security services by using *The Murder of Roger Ackroyd* and *The Mysterious Affair at Styles* to complete an elaborate disguise by using the alias 'Roger Styles'.

STRANGER THAN FICTION

At an inquest held in Coventry in November 1985, it was alleged that a killer was walking free because the only witness had changed his statement and told lies in a case where every possible suspect was known but difficult to determine, as in Agatha Christie's 'locked' or 'sealed room' murder mysteries, such as *Hercule Poirot's Christmas*.

Joe Jenkins, age twenty-two, had died during a drinking session at the home of his friend, Hugh Barclay. Two other men were present, David Cassidy and Peter McMahon. The latter told the jury that an argument over cannabis had broken out between the other three and they went into the kitchen. Shortly afterwards, Joe Jenkins returned with blood pumping from a chest wound that caused his death. The police investigation was hampered by McMahon, who then made two different statements accusing first one and then the other of his drinking companions of the crime. The jury returned a verdict of unlawful killing after hearing the coroner state, 'The story you have heard today has every ingredient of a fictional film or novel'. This view was shared by the solicitor acting on behalf of the deceased man's family, who accused McMahon of deliberately lying so that the killer could not be brought to justice: 'I do not know who is the murderer but there is a murderer in this case and I submit that you do. It is rather like the "sealed room" in Agatha Christie... You know who it was that killed that man'.

25

DAME MARGARET RUTHERFORD

Murder Most Foul

I never really wanted to play Miss Marple. I have always hated violence of any kind and murder in particular.

Margaret Rutherford (1972)

Oscar-winner Dame Margaret Rutherford (1892–1972), the well-loved 'spaniel-jowled' actress of whom acid-tongued critic Kenneth Tynan once affectionately observed, 'The unique thing about Ms Rutherford is that she can act with her chins alone' was the niece of Sir Joshua Benn and the cousin of politician Tony Benn, but throughout her life hid a terrible secret about her family's past. In her autobiography, completed shortly before her death, she glossed over the fate of her parents by simply commenting, 'My father died in tragic circumstances soon after my mother, and so I became an orphan'. Behind this fabricated understatement lay the fact that she was tormented by a grisly murder, far more bloody than any she was to investigate in her later role as Agatha Christie's fictional sleuth Miss Marple.

Ten years before Margaret's birth her father, William Rutherford Benn, who had recently been released from an asylum where he had received lengthy treatment for mental health problems, suffered a complete psychotic breakdown and battered his clergyman father's head to a pulp with a chamber pot before making a vain bid to end his own life by slashing his throat with a knife. After spending seven years in Broadmoor, the recovered patient was discharged into the care of his devoted wife, Florence. Changing their surname from Benn to Rutherford, the family made a new start in India soon after their only child, Margaret, was born, but when the infant was aged three her depressive mother hanged herself from a tree in the garden of their home in Madras. Returning to England, the grief-stricken husband was re-admitted permanently to Broadmoor. Young Margaret was then raised in London by a kindly aunt who thought it best to shield her from the terrible truth of family murder, madness and suicide by allowing her to believe that both parents were dead. At the age of twelve, Margaret learned the terrible truth from her aunt after the shocked young girl answered the door to a dishevelled man who delivered a message from her father purportedly sending his love. These horrifying revelations precipitated bouts of depressive illness brought on by an irrational fear that her mad father might escape and harm her.

As an adult, Margaret earned a living by teaching the piano and giving elocution lessons before turning to professional acting at the age of thirty-three. Finally realising a long-held ambition to join the Old Vic Co., she fell in love with fellow actor Stringer Davis, who cared for his ailing mother for a further fifteen years before popping the question; the devoted couple eventually married when the groom was forty-six and the bride fifty-three.

Margaret Rutherford gave several memorable stage and film performances during the 1930s before winning a special place in the hearts of cinema audiences as the bicycle-riding medium in Noel Coward's *Blithe Spirit* in 1945. That same year, the actress made her first appearance in an Agatha Christie work in the touring company of the stage hit *Appointment with Death*. It was over fifteen years later that she accepted an offer from MGM to play Miss Marple in *Murder She Said* (1961), loosely adapted from the murder mystery *4.50 From Paddington* (1957). Fully aware of the unsympathetic treatment that her novels were to receive at the hands of the producers, a resigned Agatha Christie watched the knockabout comedy at the ABC Cinema, Torquay, and wrote to her agent: 'Don't think I'm upset by *Murder She Said*. I'm not. It's more or less what I expected all along'. Agatha was shocked further when a Poirot case, *After the Funeral*, (1953) was converted into a vehicle for Miss Marple in the movie *Murder At the Gallop* (1963). The third outing caused even more consternation when another Poirot novel, *Mrs McGinty's Dead* (1952), was converted into a horrendous title the author had conceived in the short story 'Mr Eastwood's Adventure' (1934), where a thriller writer submits a story to a publisher predicting he will probably change it to 'something rotten' like 'Murder Most Foul'. Despite her objections to the next production, Agatha Christie suffered her worst indignity when the scriptwriters invented a totally original storyline for the final film of the series, *Murder Ahoy!*, released in 1964.

Agatha Christie watched the film during a special pre-release screening in Torquay.

Although the creator's misgivings at the distortion of her characters and plots were understandable, the films proved extremely popular at the box office and were well received by reviewers. Alexander Walker in the *Evening Standard* praised the star's performance:

> Margaret Rutherford fills the spinster's tweeds of the renowned detective Miss Marple splendidly. She is hugely enjoyable. With chin wagging like a windsock on an airfield and eyes that are deceptively guileless, she clumps her way through lines, situations and disguises that would bunker an actress of less imperial aplomb.

Rutherford recalled in her autobiography how Christie had reacted to her casting:

> I didn't know it at the time, but she was not keen on me playing Miss Marple. It was not a question of my acting, just that I didn't look at all like her idea of the detective. She saw her as a kind of fragile, pink-and-white lady, not physically like me at all! But when we met face to face on the set of *Murder She Said*, we instantly clicked and became friends. We became admirers of each other's work – hers is the world of the pen, and mine is of speech. Agatha even dedicated to me one of her Miss Marple books, *The Mirror Crack'd From Side to Side*.

Although there is no doubt that the author's gracious dedication was genuine, the book itself, featuring a series of murders on a film set, seemingly reflects the author's unflattering view of a film industry riddled with neurotics, egomaniacs, backstabbers and blackmailers.

26

ROY JAMES

At Bertram's Hotel

Oh well, those days don't seem to last when you're living hard and fast,
And life is sweet all down the line:
But when you're counting stars looking through them prison bars,
Thirty years is a long, long time.

Song chorus, *The Great Train Robbery* (1964)

The Great Train Robbery of 1963 was still fresh in the public mind when Agatha Christie wrote *At Bertram's Hotel* (1965). The novel features Miss Marple, who is staying at a restored London hotel which, she discovers, is also the headquarters of a criminal mastermind and his gang that includes a jet-setting racing driver who handles a getaway car in the 'Irish Mail train robbery'. This character was doubtless inspired by a real-life thief with a talent for racing, Roy James, who played a leading role in the most audacious heist of the twentieth century.

Long before his involvement in the infamous train robbery, Roy James had served periods of imprisonment for theft, often using the proceeds to fund his involvement in motorsport where he showed great promise and often lined up on the grid with the likes of future Grand Prix World Champions Jack Brabham, Denny Hulme and Jackie Stewart. While competing in Monte Carlo in 1962, he and an accomplice, Mickey Ball, also stole £144,000 worth of jewellery and on their return to England took part in a daylight robbery at Heathrow Airport, stealing a payroll protected by an armoured car. James needed all of his motoring skills to escape from the scene of the crime in one

Wanted

. Bucks., Aylesbury Co.—ROBBERY, 3 a.m. 8th inst., at Cheddington, vide Case 42
22-8-63. Stopped express train, attacked driver, entered travelling post office attached
to train and stole 128 post bags containing about 2½ million pounds in currency (about
£20,000 in Scottish and Irish notes). BRUCE RICHARD REYNOLDS, alias RAYMOND
ETTRIDGE and GEORGE RACHEL, C.R.O. No. 41212-48, b. London 7-9-31, motor
dealer/antique dealer, 6ft. 1in., c. fresh (slightly suntanned), h. lt. brown, e. grey
(wears horn rimmed or rimless spectacles), fairly well spoken, slight cleft in chin,
scar l. eyelid and cheek and rt. forearm. Cons. for larceny, assault on police, receiving,
causing g.b.h. with intent, shop, house, workshopbreaking, etc. at Ongar and M.P.
(C.O., C-8, C, F, L, P and W). Last, 30-5-63—fined. Is the holder of Passport No.
C.206103, issued at Marseilles, France and during the past year has visited Gibraltar,
Spain, Monte Carlo, Paris, North Africa. Represents he is in business as an antique

Bruce Richard Reynolds (photograph taken 1960)

A 'wanted' poster for Bruce Reynolds, who was captured in Torquay.

of two stolen Jaguars. While exiting through a gate in the airport's perimeter fence, he bounced off an Austin A40 trying to block his way; then, once on the main road, he balked traffic in the middle of an intersection, allowing his mate Mickey Ball to catch up and pass through a red light. In the ensuing investigation, Scotland Yard's Flying Squad quickly rounded up James and Ball, suspecting that they had orchestrated the daring getaway. A confession was extracted from Ball, who was jailed, but the case against James collapsed and he used his share of the spoils to purchase a top of the range racing car to enter a Formula Junior race, which he won in 1963.

The airport robbery had netted the gang £62,000, but the same 'firm' set its sights much higher for the next job, when leader Bruce Reynolds meticulously devised a plan to hit the Edinburgh to London night train carrying £2.6million in used bank notes, on their way to be destroyed at the Royal Mint. On 7 August 1963, the train was duly stopped by rigging a railway signal located on an isolated stretch of track at Cheddington, near Leighton Buzzard. The cab was stormed and the driver, Jack Mills, coshed over the head for initially refusing to move the train along the track to the waiting vehicles. Once this manoeuvre had been completed by the semi-concussed driver, a human chain was formed to load 150 moneybags onto an old Army truck. On this occasion, fast driving skills were not required as Roy James sedately transported some of his accomplices the short distance to a rented farmhouse at the wheel of a Land Rover.

Like a scene from an Ealing comedy, the jubilant crooks counted their ill-gotten gains and passed the time by playing Monopoly with the stolen banknotes – carelessly leaving their fingerprints on the board. When the police located the gang's hideout at Leatherslade Farm, they found an embarrassment of evidence and made short work of rounding up the majority of the culprits. James went into hiding but was caught early in December after failing to make his escape with a rooftop dash and a daring 30ft leap to the ground, where the police were waiting to apprehend him. Savage sentences were handed out at the trial of the train robbers with seven of them – Ronnie Biggs, Gordon Goody, Robert Welch, Thomas Wisbey, James Hussey, Charley Wilson and Roy James – receiving terms of thirty years. His dream of becoming a top racing driver finally over, James became the first train robber to be released on parole in 1975, only to discover that a friend he had entrusted with his share of the money had spent it all while he was in prison.

When *At Bertram's Hotel* was published in 1965, the Great Train Robbery was still hot news with the recent high-profile prison escapes by Charley Wilson and Ronnie Biggs, whilst criminal mastermind Bruce Reynolds remained at large until an international manhunt came to an end in November 1968. He was also sentenced to thirty years imprisonment after being arrested in a dawn raid mounted by the Flying Squad in Torquay. For the previous two months, the career criminal had revisited the resort where he had spent childhood holidays with his parents. Accompanied by his wife, Frances, and their six-year-old son, Nicholas, they resided at a rented luxury villa with panoramic views of Torbay. Reynolds planned to move to New Zealand, but after five years on the run with periods spent in Canada and Mexico, his share of the bank loot had dwindled from £150,000 to just £5,000. Ten days before his capture, Reynolds had a slight brush with the law for parking too close to a zebra crossing. A policeman asked him to produce his driving documents at the local police station and Britain's most wanted man calmly took his son along with him and was not recognised during the routine check. Using a false name, the robber had recently taken a driving test at nearby Newton Abbot and passed despite his nervousness when the examiner revealed that he had previously been a member of the Flying Squad. During their brief stay, the Reynolds were also members of Torquay Library, enrolling under their current alias 'Miller', which coincidentally was the maiden name of the town's famous crime author, Agatha Christie!

27

LORD MOUNTBATTEN

The Murder of Roger Ackroyd

I do not mind death as long it is reasonably peaceful and satisfying death.

Lord Mountbatten (BBC interview, 1979)

In 1974, Agatha Christie made her final public appearance at the London premiere of *Murder on the Orient Express*, attended by Queen Elizabeth, one of many members of the royal family said to be avid readers of Christie. The author was escorted to the glittering cinematic event by Lord Louis Mountbatten (1900-1979). The revered royal figure, who was the great-grandson of Queen Victoria and the great uncle of the present heir to the throne, the Prince of Wales, had acted as an emissary on behalf of his son-in-law, film producer Lord John Brabourne (1924-2005), and gently persuaded the reluctant author to give her consent to the project. It was well known that Agatha Christie had little faith in the film industry's ability to do her stories justice and she had previously only enjoyed Billy Wilder's adaptation of *Witness for the Prosecution* (1957). The decision to give the go-ahead to Lord Brabourne and his co-producer Richard Goodwin heralded a whole new era of lavish Agatha Christie films brought to the screen. The first in the series, starring Albert Finney as Hercule Poirot, was nominated for six Oscars, and in a star-studded cast Ingrid Bergman received the award for Best Supporting Actress.

Following the death of Poirot's creator in 1976, Peter Ustinov took over the role of the detective for a further three films: *Death on the Nile* (1978), *Evil Under the Sun* (1981) and *Appointment with Death* (1987). During this period, violent deaths were suffered by Mountbatten and members of the Brabourne family who were victims of a despicable act of terrorism committed in Ireland by the Provisional IRA.

In August 1979, the Mountbatten-Brabourne family took their annual one-month holiday at a castle in the fishing village of Mullaghmore, Donegal. On Monday 27 August, the party boarded the *Shadow V* for a relaxing cruise along the coast, unaware that Provo Thomas McMahon had sneaked aboard the boat and planted a remote-controlled bomb. The terrorist then stationed himself on a cliff overlooking the harbour and waited for his chance to detonate the charge and cause carnage. Shortly before noon the craft set off to inspect lobster pots that Lord Mountbatten had placed earlier. Suddenly, a terrific explosion blew the boat into smithereens and all seven occupants were hurled into the sea. Local boatmen rushed to the spot and fished out Lord Mountbatten, whose legs had been almost torn off by the blast, and he died within minutes. Doctors worked throughout the night in a vain attempt to save the life of Lord Brabourne's mother, Dowager Lady Brabourne, while her grandson Nicholas and an Ulster boat boy Paul Maxwell also died, having been found floating face down in the bloodstained water. The only survivors to recover from their serious injuries were Lord Brabourne, his wife Patricia, and their son, Nicholas's identical twin brother, Timothy.

The IRA triumphantly issued a sickening statement claiming credit for the outrage: 'The IRA claim responsibility for the execution of Lord Mountbatten. This operation is one of the discriminate ways we can bring to the attention of the English people the continuing occupation of our country'. Three hours after the murder, Thomas McMahon was arrested at a roadblock. Evidence of nitro-glycerine and flakes of paint from *Shadow V* were found on the killer's clothing, and he was convicted of the assassination and sentenced to life imprisonment. He was released in 1998 as part of the Ulster agreement that restored peace to the province.

In his entry for *Who's Who*, Lord Mounbatten conceded, 'I am the most conceited man I know'. Another proud boast of his concerned his involvement in coming up with the key element for the ending used in Agatha Christie's masterpiece, *The Murder of Roger Ackroyd* (1926), an idea that had also been mooted by her brother-in-law James Watts. In response to Lord Mountbatten's advice, Agatha replied that 'the idea was most ingenious' and, in response to his request many years later, she sent a copy of the book with a handwritten inscription: 'To Lord Mountbatten in grateful remembrance of a letter he wrote to me forty-five years ago which contained the suggestion which I subsequently used in a book called *The Murder of Roger Ackroyd*'. Her solution to the mystery is the most controversial of the brilliant surprise endings for which she became famous and it instantly elevated

Lord Mountbatten.

her to the front rank of writers. Although the book was Agatha Christie's first big seller, some readers and reviewers felt aggrieved that her choice of the narrator as the murderer had broken the unwritten rules of crime fiction. These 'rules' were addressed two years later when the Detection Club was formed by writers to maintain high standards about the use of evidence. Agatha Christie became a member of the association whose authority came too late to prevent the clever and perfectly acceptable deception, for whom the author generously acknowledged the role of her co-conspirator Lord Mountbatten: 'Thank you for presenting me with a first-class idea – no one else ever has'.

28

SIR PETER USTINOV

Evil Under the Sun

I didn't think I would end my life playing endless Poirots... it's a character performance because he seems to get his kicks in life by lip reading at a range of two hundred yards.

Sir Peter Ustinov (*Time*, 1999)

Once dubbed 'the son of Orson Welles' – another *enfant terrible* blessed with genius who enjoyed huge success but never realised his true potential – Sir Peter Ustinov (1921-2004) had an early ambition to become a great writer and the young author was compared favourably with Chekhov, Noel Coward, J.B. Priestley and George Bernard Shaw. However, due to the splendid opportunities that continually presented themselves to utilise his great diversity of talents, he never produced the literary masterpiece expected of him. The consolations were considerable in an extraordinary, multi-faceted career in the world of popular entertainment as a novelist, playwright, scriptwriter, producer, director and superb actor. He garnered two Oscars for supporting roles in the films *Spartacus* (1960) and *Topkapi* (1964), although his greatest acting fame was earned for his portrayal of Agatha Christie's Hercule Poirot.

In all, Ustinov made six appearances as the fictional sleuth, with acclaimed performances in three star-studded films, *Death on the Nile* (1978), *Evil Under the Sun* (1981) and *Appointment with Death* (1987), plus three full-length television dramas, *Thirteen at Dinner* (1985), *Dead Man's Folly* (1986) and *Murder in Three Acts* (1986). During this memorable phase of his career, the actor also found time to make award-winning television documentaries.

Burgh Island, the setting for the novel *Evil Under the Sun*.

While on one such assignment, he was present at an assassination that shook the world.

While producing a television series, *Peter Ustinov's People*, in 1984, the presenter journeyed to Delhi to conduct an interview with Indian Prime Minister Indira Gandhi. On the morning of 31 October, he was waiting in the garden to greet the premier as she walked the short distance from her official residence when the leader was attacked and died in a hail of bullets. The horrified Ustinov and his film crew heard the shooting as one of the victim's most trusted security guards, Beant Singh, drew a revolver and fired three shots at point blank range into the body of Mrs Gandhi. As she slumped to the ground another guard, Satwant Singh, pulled an automatic weapon from his shoulder and pumped its entire contents of thirty bullets into the prostrate leader. At least seven bullets penetrated the abdomen, three her chest, and one her heart. The two murderers then calmly dropped their weapons and surrendered, but were shot dead as they were taken into custody after allegedly attempting to escape. Only the day before, Indira Gandhi had evidently experienced a premonition of her tragic fate. Members of her party were startled at emotional remarks she made whilst addressing a mammoth public gathering: 'I am not interested in a long life. I am not afraid of these things. I don't mind if my life goes in the service of this nation. If I die today, every drop of my blood will invigorate the nation'.

In Ustinov's second Christie film, *Evil Under the Sun*, it is revealed that actress Arlena Stuart was acquitted of poisoning her first husband with arsenic. To develop this aspect of the plot, Agatha Christie drew on the celebrated case of American Florence Maybrick. She was charged with murder when it was discovered that she had recently purchased a large quantity of arsenic-treated flypapers and written a compromising letter to her lover saying that her husband 'is sick unto death'.

Cotton merchant James Maybrick married seventeen-year-old Southern belle Florence Chandler in 1881. After living in the USA for three years, the Maybricks returned to England and took up residence at Battlecrease House in Liverpool. The couple had two children before matrimonial difficulties surfaced. It came as a surprise to Florence to discover that her spouse was still seeing and maintaining a long-term lover, who had also borne him children. The cheated woman promptly gained revenge by finding comfort in the arms of her husband's friend and business associate Alfred Brierley. In March 1889, the hypocritical Maybrick exploded with fury when he found out about his wife's affair and during a heated exchange gave her a black eye, then drew up a new will excluding her as a beneficiary, before a sudden illness brought about his death on 11 May.

Although the evidence against Florence Maybrick seemed damning, especially the flypapers which she claimed were boiled to make an arsenical cosmetic preparation, the defence contended that the deceased had been in the habit of self-administering arsenic as an aphrodisiac, which accounted

The trial
of Florence
Maybrick.

for the traces of poison found in his system. This was confirmed by a post-mortem that found arsenic in the liver, kidney and intestines, though none in the heart or blood, which would have indicated that the dead man consumed a lethal dose of poison. However, the court was totally unsympathetic with a woman who admitted adultery and she was sentenced to death. Upon appeal the Home Secretary and the Lord Chancellor concluded 'that the evidence clearly establishes that Mrs Maybrick administered poison to her husband with intent to murder; but that there is ground for reasonable doubt whether the arsenic so administered was in fact the cause of death'. Acting on their recommendation, Queen Victoria reluctantly exercised the royal prerogative for the death penalty to be commuted to life imprisonment, commenting through her secretary 'the only regret she feels is that so wicked a woman should escape by a mere legal quibble'.

STRANGER THAN FICTION

In 1962, fifteen-year-old Graham Young confessed to attempted murder having administered poison to his father, sister and a school friend, then spent nine years in Broadmoor. Despite being diagnosed with a psychopathic disorder, the patient was freed on licence; however, his obsession with poisons compelled him to commit murder and he received a sentence of life imprisonment in June 1972.

Unbelievably, following his release in 1971, Young was helped by the probation service to obtain work as an assistant storekeeper in a photographic laboratory at Bovingdon, Hertfordshire, where he was given ready access to poisons. Carefully selecting victims among his work colleagues, he liberally dosed their tea or coffee with thallium or antimony and kept meticulous notes of his experiments in a 'diary of death'. At first the spate of illnesses, caused by what was thought to be a mystery 'bug' in the factory, bewildered doctors. It was not until the death of two men, Robert Egle and Frederick Biggs, that a pathologist had his suspicions aroused through reading about the effects of thallium poisoning in Agatha Christie's novel *The Pale Horse* (1961).

Young died of a heart attack in his cell in Parkhurst Prison in 1990, at the age of forty-two, and the man dubbed 'The Teacup Poisoner' inspired the black comedy film *The Young Poisoner's Handbook* (1995).

29

VANESSA REDGRAVE

Agatha

'Petronella will be there' is an affectionate glance at Vanessa Redgrave... the most prominent member of the Socialist Workers Party at demos.

Christie biographer Martin Fido on a quote from *Passenger to Frankfurt*

Agatha Christie's personal account of her life was published a year after her death in *An Autobiography* (1977). Despite writing frankly about the breakdown of her first marriage, she chose not to discuss the mystery of her subsequent eleven-day disappearance in December 1926. The decision not to mention this aspect of her past only increased speculation and led to a stream of published investigations and theories to rival the myths surrounding Jack the Ripper and the Loch Ness Monster.

The first book to emerge about the case of the missing author was 'an imaginary solution to an authentic mystery' by Kathleen Tynan in *Agatha: A Mystery Novel* (1978). Several months before the work was published, it was announced that it was to be adapted into a film produced by David Puttnam. The news brought an indignant response from Agatha's daughter, Rosalind, who wrote a letter to *The Times* complaining that the family had not been consulted about the forthcoming 'fairytale':

It is, however, the idea of the positive identification of my parents – both in the proposed title of the film Agatha, and also presumably in the names of characters in an admitted work of fiction – that I find particularly objectionable and morally beneath contempt.

A portrait of Agatha Christie published during the hunt for her in 1926.

Kathleen Tynan dedicated the book to her husband, controversial theatre critic Kenneth Tynan. The couple had themselves been involved in a divorce scandal when Kathleen abandoned her marriage to set up home with Tynan, then became his second wife when she was six months pregnant. In 1967, the couple were married before a New York Justice of the Peace. During the ceremony, star guest Marlene Dietrich, who ten years earlier had played the role of Christine Vole in the acclaimed film production of the Agatha Christie play *Witness for the Prosecution*, attempted to discreetly back across the office in order to close the doors that had been left ajar, causing the judge to briefly interrupt the marriage vows by issuing a warning: 'And do you, Kenneth, take Kathleen for your lawful wedded – I wouldn't stand with your ass to an open door in this office lady – wife to have and to hold?'

A theatre critic famed for his vitriolic reviews in the same mould as Kenneth Tynan, is the central character in another work that shamelessly exploited the reputation of the recently deceased 'Queen of Crime'. First produced in 1978, *Who Killed 'Agatha' Christie?*, a play by Tudor Gates, toured the provinces before opening in October at the Ambassadors Theatre, London. As reviewer Ned Chaillet wryly observed in *The Times*: 'Of course, the Agatha Christie referred to is not the sweet old lady who wrote fantasies of murder, but really Arthur Christie, the dramatic critic who butchered plays and players with his criticism and had a secret homosexual life. Agatha is a term of endearment'. In the story, playwright John Terry (originally played by James Bolam), whose productions have been malevolently savaged by the critic, lures Arthur, aka Agatha, (Gerald Flood) to a rented flat to listen to recorded sex acts between the critic's boyfriend and the playwright's wife. John Terry's intent is to have his revenge by killing the love cheats and his poison pen friend in this 'thrilling psychological drama with a devilish dash of macabre humour'.

In Kathleen Tynan's *Agatha*, a highly imaginative reconstruction of the famous author's disappearance, the missing woman is not suffering from amnesia but, distraught over her husband's other woman, plans to commit suicide at a hotel by means of electrocution in the hydro-bath. By utilising her crime writing skills, the death is to be staged to appear like murder at the hands of Archie's 'other woman'. Starring in the title role of the film version *Agatha* (1979) was Oscar-winning actress Vanessa Redgrave (b. 1937), who five years earlier had appeared as governess Mary Debenham in *Murder on the Orient Express*.

A prominent political activist, Redgrave donated her £40,000 fee for the part of 'Agatha' to the Workers' Revolutionary Party. In 2003, she hit the headlines by providing a £50,000 surety to support Akhmed Zakayev, a Chechen separatist campaigner. He was fighting a legal action to extradite him to Russia, where he was accused of thirteen serious offences including: armed rebellion, kidnapping two priests, torturing a suspected informer, taking part in a firing squad, and the murder of 300 troops and twelve civilians. The former Culture Minister and actor was likened to Islamic terrorist leader Osama Bin Laden and said to be implicated in the 2002 Moscow theatre siege. This tragic episode resulted in the death of 130 people when armed Chechen rebels, with explosives strapped to their waists, held a theatre audience of 800 people to ransom, demanding that Russian forces be withdrawn from their homeland. Three days later, when negotiations had failed to bring about a peaceful solution to the crisis, Russian troops stormed the building after sedative gas was pumped into the theatre in an attempt to render the terrorists unconscious. The military intervention resulted in the deaths of eighty members of the public and all fifty of the suicide bombers. At a hearing at Bow Street Court, a judge rejected Russia's request for extradition on the grounds of fears that Zakeyev faced torture if he was forced to return to face questioning and because the crimes allegedly involving the defendant were committed during an 'internal armed conflict'. Vanessa Redgrave pronounced that the political asylum seeker was a highly respected actor in his home state, 'not a warlord and not a terrorist'.

Mass murder in a theatre had previously been attempted in South Africa during the showing of Agatha Christie's play *The Hollow*, in which glamorous actress Veronica Crane attempts to rekindle a romance with former fiancé Dr John Christow. When the ex-lovers meet at a secret rendezvous, the physician is shot dead and the killer later dies drinking tea laced with poison. Under the headline, 'A Real Life Whodunnit', the *Sunday Express* reported in March 1984:

A stage hand has been charged with attempted murder in a real-life 'whodunnit' backstage at a Johannesburg theatre where an Agatha Christie play was showing. The man was charged after poison was found in the cast's kettle only fifteen minutes before the villain in *The Hollow* 'died' on stage… of poisoning.

30

AGATHA CHRISTIE

Ordeal by Innocence

It is a case where the innocent suffer most horribly for sins they have never committed. They live in a haze of publicity, acquaintances and friends look at them curiously; there are continually autograph hunters, curious idle crowds. Any decent happy private life is made impossible for them.

Agatha Christie on the Croydon Murders (The *Sunday Chronicle* 1929)

Throughout her long writing career, Agatha Christie had an ongoing fascination with the Bravo Case and the Croydon Murders – unsolved true crimes that formed the premise of one of her best detective novels, *Ordeal by Innocence* (1958), the story of a family thrown into turmoil when they are forced to consider which one of them might be a murderer.

The first mystery that took the author's interest was the case of barrister Charles Bravo, who married wealthy young widow Florence Ricardo after a whirlwind courtship in December 1875. The newlyweds lived at The Priory in Balham with Florence's companion, widow Jane Cox, who witnessed arguments between the couple over her mistress's association with a former lover, Dr James Gully. After four months of married life, Charles was taken ill after eating dinner with the two women. He died three days later after being attended by his love rival, Dr Gully. A post-mortem concluded that he had been poisoned by a single dose of antimony and an inquest returned an open verdict, although it was widely believed that the victim had committed suicide as Jane Cox testified that he had told her, 'I have taken poison for Dr Gully. Don't tell Florence'. However, revelations in the press about

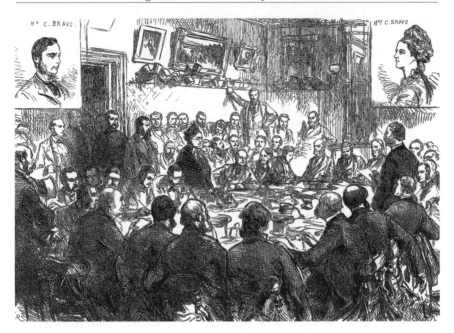

Jane Cox is questioned at the inquest into the death of Charles Bravo.

the widow's relationship with the family doctor and the fact that Jane Cox had been on bad terms with the deceased resulted in a second inquest being held, which virtually developed into a trial of the two women. This time, the verdict was 'wilful murder', although there was insufficient evidence to place the blame against anyone. By this time, Florence and Jane were no longer friends and a contemporary broadsheet ballad summed up the popular belief that a cunning wife had laced her husband's wine and cast suspicion on her companion:

> When lovely woman stoops to folly
> And finds her husband in the way,
> What charm can soothe her melancholy?
> What art can turn him into clay?
>
> The only means her aim to cover,
> And save herself from prison locks,
> And repossess her ancient lover
> Are Burgundy and Mrs Cox!

A character in *Ordeal by Innocence* comments on the unresolved aspects of the case:

And so Florence Bravo, abandoned by her family, died alone of drink, and Mrs Cox, ostracised, and with three little boys, lived to be an old woman with most of the people she knew believing her to be a murderer, and Dr Gully was ruined professionally and socially. Someone was guilty – and got away with it. But the others were innocent – and didn't get away with anything.

In a letter to Francis Wyndham, editor of the *Sunday Times Magazine*, written in 1968, Agatha dismissed the case against the two women as Florence Bravo 'had the money', whilst Mrs Cox was 'an obvious suspect at first hand, but not when you look into it'. The crime writer firmly believed it was Dr Gully who killed Charles Bravo: 'I've always felt that he was the only person who had an overwhelming motive and who was the right type: exceedingly competent, successful, and always considered above suspicion'.

In the second case that attracted Agatha Christie's interest, a serial murderer escaped detection in Croydon when three members of the same family died of poisoning between April 1928 and March 1929. Retired colonial civil servant Edmund Duff passed away after a brief illness, considered to be caused by a heart condition. Suspicions about his death were only aroused when his daughter-in-law Vera Sidney and her mother, Violet Sidney, died within a month of each other. All three bodies were then exhumed and found to contain arsenic. It was thought that poison had been administered to the victims in food or medicine by a close family member. Although there was insufficient evidence to bring a prosecution, the chief suspect was Grace Duff, widow of Edmund, who was alleged to have wanted rid of her husband as she was having an affair with a doctor, while the female relatives were murdered for financial gain.

In her letter published by the *Sunday Times* in 1968, Agatha Christie revealed that she was unable to offer a solution to the mystery but would continue her investigation into 'whodunnit' beyond the grave: 'All I can say is, dear Francis Wyndham, that if I die and go to heaven, or the other place, and so it happens that the Public Prosecutor of that time is also there, I shall beg him to reveal the secret to me'.

BIBLIOGRAPHY
AND SOURCES

General Sources

Agatha Christie Collection, Nos 1-85 (Agatha Christie Ltd, a Chorion company, 2001-2005)

Bunson, Matthew, *The Complete Christie Encyclopedia* (London, Pocket Books, 2000)

Ellis, Arthur, *An Historical Survey of Torquay* (Subscribers Edition, 1930)

Harris, Martin, *The Official Guide to Agatha Christie in Devon* (Produced under licence from Agatha Christie Ltd) (Paignton, Creative Media Publishing, 2009)

Matthews, H.C.G., and Harris, Brian (Eds), *Oxford Dictionary of National Biography* (Oxford, Oxford University Press, 2004)

Morselt, Ben, *An A-Z of the Novels and Short Stories of Agatha Christie* (Bushey, Phoenix Publishing Associates, 1985)

Norman, Andrew, *Agatha Christie* (Andover, Pitkin Publishing, 2009)

Sanders, Dennis, and Lovallo, Len, *The Agatha Christie Companion* (London, W.H. Allen, 1985)

Sova, Dawn B., *Agatha Christie A-Z* (New York, Checkmark Books, 2000)

Toye, Randall, *The Agatha Christie Who's Who* (London, Frederick Muller Ltd, 1980)

20th Century News (Plymouth, Western Morning News Co. Ltd, 2000)

Sources by Chapter

1 *Agatha Christie: 'The Queen of Crime'*

Morgan, Janet, 'Christie, Dame Agatha Mary Clarissa, 1890-1976' in *Oxford Dictionary of National Biography* (Oxford, Oxford University Press, 2004)

Christie, Agatha, *An Autobiography* (London, Collins, 1977)

Journals and Magazines:
Herald Express
Western Morning News

2 Jack the Ripper: Cat Among the Pigeons

Davenport-Hines, Richard, 'Jack the Ripper' in *Oxford Dictionary of National Biography* (Oxford, Oxford University Press, 2004)

Holgate, Mike, *Jack the Ripper: The Celebrity Suspects* (Stroud, The History Press, 2008)

Journals and Magazines:

The Agatha Christie Collection No. 5, *The ABC Murders* (Agatha Christie Ltd, 2001)

The Agatha Christie Collection No. 43, *Cat Among the Pigeons* (Agatha Christie Ltd, 2003)

3 Lady Nancy Astor: Appointment With Death

Osbourne, Charles, *The Life and Crimes of Agatha Christie* (London, HarperCollins, 2000)

Pugh, Martin, 'Viscountess Nancy Witcher Astor' in *Oxford Dictionary of National Biography* (Oxford, Oxford University Press, 2004)

Journals and Magazines:

The Agatha Christie Collection No. 22, Appointment With Death, Agatha Christie Ltd., 2002

4 Lizzie Borden: After the Funeral

Gaute, J.H.H. & Odell, Robin, *The Murderer's Who's Who* (London, Pan Books, 1980)

Journals and Magazines:
Illustrated Police News
Torquay Times
The Times

The Agatha Christie Collection No. 4, *And Then There Were None* (Agatha Christie Ltd, 2001)

The Agatha Christie Collection No. 39, *Ordeal by Innocence* (Agatha Christie Ltd, 2003)

The Agatha Christie Collection No. 58, *Sleeping Murder* (Agatha Christie Ltd, 2004)

5 Sir Arthur Conan Doyle: The Hound of Death

Edwards, Owen Dudley, 'Sir Arthur Ignatius Conan Doyle' in *Oxford Dictionary of National Biography* (Oxford, Oxford University Press, 2004)

Garrick-Steele, Rodger, *The House of the Baskervilles* (Indiana, USA, Authorhouse, 2003)

Holgate, Mike. *Jack the Ripper: The Celebrity Suspects* (Stroud, The History Press 2008)

Kalush, William, and Sloman, Larry R., *The Secret Life of Houdini* (New York, Pocket Books, 2007)

JOURNALS AND MAGAZINES:
The Times

6 Oscar Wilde: A Woman of No Importance

Edwards, Owen Dudley, 'Wilde, Oscar Fingal O'Flahertie Wills' in Oxford *Dictionary of National Biography* (Oxford, Oxford University Press, 2004)

Bentley, Joyce, *The Importance of Being Constance* (London, Hale, 1983)

Hart-Davis, Rupert, *More Letters of Oscar Wilde* (London, Murray, 1985)

Hyde, Montgomery H., *Famous Trials 7: Oscar Wilde* (Harmondsworth, Middlesex, Penguin Books, 1962)

JOURNALS AND MAGAZINES:
The Theatre
The Times
Torquay Times
South Devon Advertiser

7 Agatha Christie: The Mysterious Affair at Styles

Christie, Agatha, *An Autobiography* (London, Collins, 1977)

Norman, Dr Andrew, *Agatha Christie: The Finished Portrait* (Stroud, Tempus Publishing Ltd, 2006)

Thompson, Laura, *Agatha Christie: An English Mystery* (London, Headline Review, 2007)

JOURNALS AND MAGAZINES:
Daily Mail
Evening News
Western Morning News

8 Dame Gracie Fields: A Murder Is Announced

Haining, Peter, *Murder in Four Acts* (London, Virgin Books, 1990)

Osbourne, Charles, *The Life and Crimes of Agatha Christie* (London, HarperCollins, 2000)

Richards, Jeffrey, 'Dame Gracie Fields', in Oxford *Dictionary of National Biography* (Oxford, Oxford University Press, 2004)

JOURNALS AND MAGAZINES:
Herald Express
New York Times
TV Guide (USA)

9 Lord Carnarvon: The Adventure of the Egyptian Tomb

Christie, Agatha, *Poirot Investigates* (London, The Bodley Head, 1924)

Carter, Howard, and Mace, A.C., *The Tomb of Tutankhamun* (London, Cassell & Co., 1923)

Furneaux, Rupert, *The World's Strangest Mysteries* (London, Odhams Press, 1961)

Fagan, Brian. 'Herbert, George Edward Stanhope Molyneaux, Fifth Earl of Carnavon' in *Oxford Dictionary of National Biography* (Oxford, Oxford University Press, 2004)

James, T.G.H., 'Howard Carter' in *Oxford Dictionary of National Biography* (Oxford, Oxford University Press, 2004)

JOURNALS AND MAGAZINES:

The Agatha Christie Collection No. 3, *Death on the Nile* (Agatha Christie Ltd, 2001)

The Agatha Christie Collection No. 71, *Poirot Investigates* (Agatha Christie Ltd, 2004)

10 Sir Humphrey Gilbert and Sir Walter Raleigh: Dead Man's Folly

Nicholls, Mark, and Williams, Penry, 'Sir Walter Raleigh' in *Oxford Dictionary of National Biography* (Oxford, Oxford University Press, 2004)

Prince, John, *Worthies of Devon* (London, Longman, 1810)

Rapple, Rory, 'Sir Humphrey Gilbert' in *Oxford Dictionary of National Biography* (Oxford, Oxford University Press, 2004)

JOURNALS AND MAGAZINES:

The Agatha Christie Collection No. 74, *The Adventure of the Christmas Pudding* (Agatha Christie Ltd, 2004)

11 Robert Graves: Towards Zero

Graves, Richard Perceval, 'Robert von Ranke Graves' in *Oxford Dictionary of National Biography* (Oxford, Oxford University Press, 2004)

Jones, Nigel, *Countdown to Valkyrie* (London, Frontline Books, 2009)

Seymour-Smith, Martin, *Robert Graves: His Life and Work* (London, Hutchinson, 1982)

Thompson, Laura, *Agatha Christie: An English Mystery* (London, Headline Review, 2007)

12 Madge Watts: The Claimant

Christie, Agatha, *An Autobiography* (London, Collins, 1977)

McWilliam, Rohan, 'Sir Henry Tichborne' in *Oxford Dictionary of National Biography* (Oxford, Oxford University Press, 2004)

JOURNALS AND MAGAZINES:

Illustrated London News

People

The Times

13 Rudyard Kipling: The House Surgeon

Carrington, Charles, *Rudyard Kipling: His Life and Work* (London, Macmillan, 1953)

Kipling, Rudyard, *Something of Myself* (London, Macmillan, 1937)

Pinney, Thomas, 'Kipling, (Joseph) Rudyard' in *Oxford Dictionary of National Biography* (Oxford, Oxford University Press, 2004)

JOURNALS AND MAGAZINES:
Torquay Times

14 Dr Crippen: Three Act Tragedy

Fido, Martin, 'Crippen, Hawley Harvey' in *Oxford Dictionary of National Biography* (Oxford, Oxford University Press, 2004)

Fido, Martin, *The World of Agatha Christie* (London, Carlton Books Ltd, 1977)

Gaute, J.H.H. & Odell, Robin, *The Murderer's Who's Who* (London, Pan Books, 1980)

JOURNALS AND MAGAZINES:
The Times
Newark Evening Star
The Agatha Christie Collection. No. 21, *Dumb Witness* (Agatha Christie Ltd, 2002)
The Agatha Christie Collection No. 35, *Mrs McGinty's Dead* (Agatha Christie Ltd, 2001)

15 Ernest Shackleton and Robert Falcon Scott: The Adventure of the Christmas Pudding

King, H.G.R., 'Robert Falcon Scott' in *Oxford Dictionary of National Biography* (Oxford, Oxford University Press, 2004)

Savours, Ann, 'Sir Ernest Henry Shackleton' in *Oxford Dictionary of National Biography* (Oxford, Oxford University Press, 2004)

Shackleton, Sir Ernest Henry, *South* (London, Heinemann, 1919)

Scott, R.F., *Scott's Last Voyage* (London, Smith, Elder & Co., 1913)

JOURNALS AND MAGAZINES:
The Agatha Christie Collection No. 39, *Ordeal by Innocence* (Agatha Christie Ltd, 2003)
The Agatha Christie Collection No. 67, *The Thirteen Problems* (Agatha Christie Ltd, 2004)

16 Billie Carleton: The Affair at the Victory Ball

Cochran, C.B., *Secrets of a Showman* (London, William Heinemann, 1925)

Hore, Philip, 'Billie Carleton' in *Oxford Dictionary of National Biography* (Oxford, Oxford University Press, 2004)

JOURNALS AND MAGAZINES:
Evening News
The Times
The Agatha Christie Collection No. 10, *The Big Four* (Agatha Christie Ltd, 2001)

17 *The Sinking of the* Lusitania*: The Secret Adversary*

Wawro, Dr Geoffrey (Ed.), *Historica: 100 Years of Our Lives and Times* (Elanora
Heights, NSW, Australia, Millennium Publishing, 2006)

Visual History of the Twentieth Century (Goldalming, Colour Direct Ltd, 1999)

JOURNALS AND MAGAZINES:
The Times
Western Morning News
The Agatha Christie Collection No. 6, *The Secret Adversary* (Agatha Christie
Ltd, 2001)

18 *Lawrence of Arabia: They Came to Baghdad*

James, Lawrence, 'Lawrence, T.E.' in *Oxford Dictionary of National Biography*
(Oxford, Oxford University Press, 2004)

Hearn, Chester G., *Spies & Espionage: A Directory* (San Diego, Thunder Bay
Press, 2006)

JOURNALS AND MAGAZINES:
The Agatha Christie Collection No. 42, *They Came to Baghdad* (Agatha
Christie Ltd, 2003)

19 *Eden Phillpotts: Peril At End House*

Christie, Agatha, *An Autobiography* (London, Collins, 1977)

Dayananda, James, 'Mary Adelaide Eden Phillpotts' in *Oxford Dictionary of
National Biography* (Oxford, Oxford University Press, 2004)

Moult, Thomas, 'Eden Phillpotts' in *Oxford Dictionary of National Biography*,
(Oxford, Oxford University Press, 2004)

Ross, A, *Reverie: An Autobiography* (London, Robert Hale, 1981)

20 *Charles Lindbergh: Murder on the Orient Express*

Caren, Eric C. (Ed.), *Crime Extra: 300 Years of Crime in North America* (New
Jersey. Castle Books, 2001)

Erwin, Douglas, *Extinction: How Life on Earth Nearly Ended 250 Million Years Ago*
(New Jersey, Princeton University Press, 2006)

Erwin, Douglas, The *Great Paleozoic Crisis: Life and Death in the Permian* (New
York, Columbia University Press, 1993)

Gaute, J.H.H. & Odell, Robin, *The Murderer's Who's Who*, (London, Pan Books,
1980)

JOURNALS AND MAGAZINES:
The Agatha Christie Collection No. 1, *Murder on the Orient Express* (Agatha
Christie Ltd, 2001)
Journals and Magazines:
Herald Express

21 Frank Vosper: Love From A Stranger
White, Patrick, *Flaws In the Glass* (London, Cape, 1981)
Website Sources:
Gay for Today
Martin Edwards's Crime Writing Blog

JOURNALS AND MAGAZINES:
Daily Mail
Daily Mirror
The Times

22 Sir Christopher Lee: Murder Is Easy
Lee, Christopher, *Lord of Misrule: The Autobiography of Christopher Lee* (London, Orion Books, 2004)
Holgate, Mike, *Murder & Crime: Devon*, (Stroud, Tempus Publishing, 2007)
Odell, Robin, *Exhumation of a Murder: The Life and Trial of Major Armstrong* (London, Harrap, 1975)

JOURNALS AND MAGAZINES:
The Agatha Christie Collection No. 58, Sleeping Murder (Agatha Christie Ltd, 2004)
The Agatha Christie Collection No. 72, Partners In Crime (Agatha Christie Ltd, 2004)

23 Dennis O'Neill: The Mousetrap
Gregg, Hubert, *Agatha Christie and All That Mousetrap*, (London, William Kimber & Co. Ltd, 1980)
Stephens, Francis (Ed.). *Theatre World Annual No. 4*, (London, Rockliffe Publishing Corporation, 1953)

JOURNALS AND MAGAZINES:
Daily Express
The Financial Times
The Times
The Agatha Christie Collection No. 54, *Lord Edgware Dies* (Agatha Christie Ltd, 2003)
The Agatha Christie Collection No. 75, *The Mousetrap* (Agatha Christie Ltd, 2004)

24 Klaus Fuchs and Bruno Pontecorvo: Destination Unknown
Flowers, Mary, 'Klaus Emil Julius Fuchs' in *Oxford Dictionary of National Biography* (Oxford, Oxford University Press, 2004)
Hearn, Chester G., *Spies & Espionage: A Directory* (San Diego, Thunder Bay Press, 2006)
Kerr, Sheila, 'Guy Francis de Money Burgess' in *Oxford Dictionary of National Biography* (Oxford, Oxford University Press, 2004)

JOURNALS AND MAGAZINES:
The Agatha Christie Collection No. 65, *Destination Unknown* (Agatha Christie
    Ltd, 2004)
The Agatha Christie Collection No. 68, *Passenger to Frankfurt* (Agatha Christie
    Ltd, 2004)

25 Dame Margaret Rutherford: Murder Most Foul
Gielgud, John, 'Dame Margaret Taylor Rutherford' in *Oxford Dictionary of
    National Biography* (Oxford, Oxford University Press, 2004)
Haining, Peter, *Murder in Four Acts* (London, Virgin Books, 1990)
Merriman, Andy, *Margaret Rutherford* (London, Aurum, 2009)
Rutherford, Margaret, *Margaret Rutherford: An Autobiography as told to Gwen
    Robyns* (London, W.H. Allen, 1972)

JOURNALS AND MAGAZINES:
Daily Mail
Evening News
Independent on Sunday
The Times

26 Roy James: At Bertram's Hotel
Reynolds, Bruce, *Autobiography of a Thief* (London, Corgi, 1995)
Crimes and Criminals (London, W. & R. Chambers Ltd, 1992)

JOURNALS AND MAGAZINES:
Herald Express
The Times
The Agatha Christie Collection No. 62, *At Bertram's Hotel* (Agatha Christie
    Ltd, 2004)

27 Lord Mountbatten: The Murder of Roger Ackroyd
Christie, Agatha, *An Autobiography* (London, Collins, 1977)
Davis, Lee, *Assassination: Twenty Assassinations That Changed the World* (Abingdon,
    Transedition Books, 1993)
Zeigler, Philip, 'Mountbatten, Earl Louis Francis Albert Victor Nicholas' in *Oxford
    Dictionary of National Biography* (Oxford, Oxford University Press, 2004)

JOURNALS AND MAGAZINES:
The Agatha Christie Collection No. 10, *The Murder of Roger Ackroyd* (Agatha
    Christie Ltd, 2001)

28 Sir Peter Ustinov: Evil Under the Sun
Bailey, Brian, 'Sir Peter Alexander Ustinov' in *Oxford Dictionary of National
    Biography* (Oxford, Oxford University Press, 2004)
Davis, Lee, *Assassination: Twenty Assassinations That Changed the World* (Abingdon,
    Transedition Books, 1993)

JOURNALS AND MAGAZINES:
Hindustan Times
Time
The Agatha Christie Collection No. 3, *Death on the Nile* (Agatha Christie Ltd, 2001)

29 *Vanessa Redgrave: Agatha*

Fido, Martin, *The World of Agatha Christie* (London, Carlton Books Ltd, 1977)
Lahr, John (Ed.), *The Diaries of Kenneth Tynan* (London, Bloomsbury, 2001)
Tynan, Kathleen, *Agatha: A Mystery Novel* (London, Weidenfield & Nicolson, 1978)

JOURNALS AND MAGAZINES:
Independent
Sunday Express
The Times

30 *Agatha Christie: Ordeal by Innocence*

Gaute, J.H.H. & Odell, Robin, *The Murderer's Who's Who*, (London, Pan Books, 1980)
Thompson, Laura, *Agatha Christie: An English Mystery* (London, Headline Review, 2007)

JOURNALS AND MAGAZINES:
Illustrated London News
Sunday Chronicle
Sunday Times
The Agatha Christie Collection No. 39, *Ordeal by Innocence* (Agatha Christie Ltd, 2003)

Other titles published by The History Press

Agatha Christie: The Finished Portrait
DR ANDREW NORMAN

When Agatha Christie, the so-called 'Queen of Crime', disappeared from her home in Sunningdale in Berkshire for eleven days on 3 December 1926, the whole nation held its breath. From a painstaking reconstruction of Agatha's movements and behaviour during those eleven days, Dr Andrew Norman is able to shed new light on what, in many ways, has remained a baffling mystery. Only now, fifty years after Agatha's death, it possible to explain fully her behaviour during that troubled time.

978 0 7524 4288 4

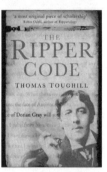

The Ripper Code
THOMAS TOUGHILL

The Ripper Code is a fascinating combination of literary and conventional detective work, which is as original as it is enthralling. After showing that the official Ripper files contain little of forensic interest, the author approaches the subject of the killer's identity from an entirely different angle – the life and works of Oscar Wilde. The author also claims that Jack the Ripper was placed in an asylum after the last murder in order to keep secret a royal indiscretion.

978 0 7524 5276 0

Murder & Crime: Devon
MIKE HOLGATE

Within these pages are accounts of Robert James Lees, the Ilfracombe spiritualist who claimed to have unmasked Jack the Ripper; Herbert Rowse Armstrong, the former Newton Abbot solicitor who remains the only member of his profession to be executed for murder; and Oscar Wilde, whose downfall was initiated by an incriminating letter sent from Babbacombe. With more than sixty illustrations, this chilling book is bound to captivate anyone interested in Devon's dark history.

978 0 7524 4504 5

Victorian CSI
WILLIAM A. GUY, DAVID FERRIER & WILLIAM R. SMITH

The first edition of William A. Guy's *Principles of Forensic Medicine* was published at the start of Victoria's reign; the final edition, from which these selections derive, was published towards the end, just a few years after the Whitechapel horrors had pushed the emerging science to the forefront of the public's consciousness. With original woodcuts, case studies and notes on identifying the corpse and walking the crime scene, *Victorian CSI* will fascinate lovers of crime fiction and of true crime alike.

978 0 7524 5513 6

Visit our website and discover thousands of other History Press books.

www.thehistorypress.co.uk